Praise for Whistling Up in Ghostland

For the Book

Ryan's storytelling gifts shine through in this writing as well as song lyrics.

> — Terry Lovelette, author of *Thoughts from a Walk, Down-Back*, and *In Praise of Eagle Mountain*

I needed a handkerchief as I read these well-written, compelling, and touching essays. Reading the stories and then hearing the songs combines for the best kind of ecstatic experience with a book!

> — Michael Caldwell, author of *The Tao of Snow*

Ryan's book fed my soul with its beautiful epiphanies. His writing is wonderfully vivid. It is the kind of writing I love. The lyrics were pure joy, the type you feel deep within your being. Just wonderful!

> — Pam C.

Beautiful, evocative writing. I love it all.

> — Fran F.

I think anyone can relate to this journey of self-discovery and all the vivid depictions of Jim's life and adventures—even if it's just to wish they had such drive to make the most of their time and pursue their passions. It made me want to live Jim's life, something out of a literary adventure, but real and incredible.

— Jamie R.

I absolutely loved being able to listen to the song after reading the story. The stories are page-turners.

— Mike K.

Ryan's writing voice is human, grounded, expressive, engaging, and more - all the things that matter.

— Yvette D.

For the *Free Now* Album and Ryan's Lyrics

Ryan writes lyrics full of romantic whimsy and themes of home and family- true roots music... in an album packed with Green Mountain talent.

— Seven Days

Ryan's songwriting tells stories that touch on spirituality, the death of loved ones, connection to land and place, and romantic love... (Free Now) is a strong album that entertains...

— Times Argus

... Ryan has a deep and active soul with the rare ability to put feelings into words. He shines in "My New Old Friend."

— Ellen S.

Emotionally powerful! The emotion I felt listening to the words of Ryan's lyrics was moving...

— Lisa Ann L.

Songs are always better if you know about the rattlesnakes and naked hippies. As I was listening, I thought the songs had a John Prine feel to them—very high praise!

— Douglas A. S.

Fun and funny, and powerful.

— Steve F.

Whistling Up In Ghostland

Essays and Songs of Adventure, Intuition, and Awakening

Jim Ryan

Bear Swamp Media

Whistling Up in Ghostland: Essays and Songs of Adventure, Intuition, and Awakening

Published by Bear Swamp Media
Wolcott, VT

Copyright ©2026 Jim Ryan. All rights reserved.

No part of this book may be reproduced in any form or by any mechanical means, including information storage and retrieval systems without permission in writing from the publisher/author, except by a reviewer who may quote passages in a review.

All images, logos, quotes, and trademarks included in this book are subject to use according to trademark and copyright laws of the United States of America.

Paperback ISBN: 979-8-9945582-0-1
Hardcover ISBN: 979-8-9945582-1-8
MUSIC / Religious / General

Cover design by Asya Blue. Copyright owned by Jim Ryan.

All rights reserved by Jim Ryan and Bear Swamp Media

Contents

*This book is dedicated to those friends and family who have
entered the spirit world and whose stories are
woven within these pages:
Eva, Max, Lydia, Grandpa John, Rita, Sean, Quinn, and Joe
—my door is always open for you to visit*

And to the "343" for their valiant sacrifice on 9/11

With Gratitude

To Joanne Breidenstein—my friend, collaborator, and editor extraordinaire; thank you for your patience, your persistence, and your time. I couldn't have done this without you!

To my devil friend Brandon Dennis—my cosmic pirate ship copilot—may the magic continue to follow us wherever we go.

To the talented musicians—Dave Keller, Lizzy Mandell, Colin McCaffrey, Carly Harvey, Scott Graner, and Jay Gleason and Zeph Courtney at Destroy Audio—thank you for turning my words and stories into stirring songs.

Thanks to my sister—Jamie Lynn Ryan at Snapshots and Silhouettes, for being an early and enthusiastic reader and for your assistance with the photos.

To Bradley Hortsman—for his diligent work in developing and maintaining my website.

My appreciation for the work of Bryan Canter at My Word Publishing, Lesley Allen at Perceptive Editing, and Asya Blue Design.

Special thanks to all my beta readers. Your thoughtful insights and support were invaluable.

And to my person, Katie, thank you for letting me be me.

I am deeply grateful to you all.

*May our intentions be visualized, then
manifested, without expectation.*

Author's Note

Music is the mystic, and song, my spirituality.

I have never considered myself a musician. My only musical claim to fame was playing the snare drum in a bagpipe band. I continue to struggle to learn how to play the guitar. But I always loved to tell stories through song lyrics. I realized over the last two decades that I had written about many of my extraordinary life experiences, not in prose, but through lyrics.

For a long time, I was incapable of fully describing these pivotal life moments, despite the enormous impact they had upon me. I was reluctant to share these events even with close friends and family. I was unable to express in words, written or verbally, what had happened. Lyrics bridged that ineffability gap. Adhering to the song verse-chorus template and imposing a rhyme scheme helped me focus my thoughts. Crafting the words to songs was my first step in processing and understanding what was happening before me, and within me.

My journey of understanding began a year before the Covid-19 pandemic struck the international community. My quest continued through the pandemic's course when I turned inward. That time of relative isolation and uncertainty provided vast context to some concepts I was trying to come to terms with, the physical, emotional, and spiritual spectrums converging in me. As I continued my practice of writing lyrics to help process my personal awakening, I embarked on a parallel track of extensive journaling and writing and later, researching to shed light on what was unfolding. Along the way, I began to find my spirituality and better understand my true self.

The essays that follow describe travel off the beaten path, openness to possibilities, natural beauty, sense of place, deep friendship, collective emotion, death, grief, self-discovery, mindfulness, presence, intuition, and personal transformation.

The significant moments described in the coming pages are accompanied by corresponding song lyrics. In some instances, the lyrics have been developed fully into songs, in collaboration with seasoned singer-songwriters. Songs are sprinkled throughout these pages, with links to the audio. Many of these songs are included in the *Free Now* album.

The album we created was pure magic. It moved many listeners, friends, family, neighbors, radio station DJs, other musicians, and complete strangers. Listeners were intrigued by the characters in the lyrics and the emotion of the music, melodies, and vocals. In some cases, they were moved to tears. They wanted to know if the stories and characters described within the songs were real. The intrigue, emotion, and interest of the listeners motivated me to write this book.

Woven into all the chapters is the influence of living on a small farm in the "southwest corner of the Northeast King-dom" of Vermont. Raising livestock and growing fruits and vegetables on the fields and harvesting firewood in the forest has deeply influenced my writing and the evolution of my spirituality. My deep connection to this land, and my sense of place within it, set the stage for many of the song lyrics. The convergence of emotion, nature, and music, shared by like-minded souls is my sweet spot and where all the magic happens.

The following pages describe some of my extraordinary life experiences, without the assistance of AI. We all have such experiences, each unique and yet universal. I am reminded of the adage "Write what you know." The following pages describe just that, what I know.

Jim Ryan—Bear Swamp Farm, Vermont

THE CURVEBALL

Saline Skies

Death Valley, California

We said goodbye to Big Pine Town with our mission declared successful. Our rental car's flat tire was plugged and our depleted provisions of food and beer replenished. As Brandon and I ascended the Inyo Mountains, we listened to our CDs on the Pathfinder's stereo, old school. Ryan Adams's twangy double album *Cold Roses* just seemed right in that moment and that landscape. We reached into our recently purchased groceries, and the road sodas began popping at midday.

Just as we crossed the Inyo Mountains, we had the urge to pull over and get out on the side of this desolate back road returning us to Death Valley and Eureka Dunes. I stood in the middle of the sun-beaten asphalt road dividing the dull brown mesquite and creosote scrub on either side, with the backdrop of the snow-covered Inyo Mountains behind me. I raised both arms up high, as if I were embracing my surroundings with all I could muster inside me. I strode over to the parked SUV as Brandon handed me a beer and a cigar. I hopped on the hood of the SUV, opened the beer, and lit up the cigar. A sensation of pure bliss filled me. Both moments were captured by Brandon's camera. We were overcome by the music and the magnificent setting. We kept the car windows open so we could continue to hear the music. We were overwhelmed with a feeling of awe and awareness. Any pre-trip stress lingering within us had been released as we embraced the breathtaking blue sky and mountain ranges stretched as far as our eyes could see. That moment we later described as "Going Over the Inyo." It resulted from "flat tire magic." Brandon proclaimed my trip nickname, Big Pine. Eighteen years later, he still calls me that. Today we call any synchronistic events "flat tire magic" and we continue to describe our consciousness shifts resulting in moments of bliss as "Going Over the Inyo."

Jim "Going Over the Inyo," part 1 (photo credit Brandon Dennis)

We had arrived in Death Valley National Park several days prior, after flying to San Diego from Burlington, Vermont. It was Brandon who initiated the idea of the trip. He was immersed in the mundane task of washing dishes in his kitchen, while lubricated with a few beers as U2's song "With or Without You" came on the radio. Brandon first taunted us with a group email inviting us to a grand adventure to one of the most inhospitable places on Earth, before calling each of us individually. We were all "in." Pat, Kevin, and I lived in Vermont and Brandon called the Catskill Mountains in New York home. Pat was at the center of our friendship web, as a college buddy of Brandon's. Brandon, my former coworker, brought me into the friend circle. Pat, in turn, brought in Kevin. We all became fast friends and bonded over our love of outdoor adventure on numerous trips from the nearby Green Mountains and Adirondacks to our trips out west to explore the national parks and forests, Bureau of Land Management properties, oceans, and mountains.

I had been a desert newbie, until Brandon introduced me to Edward Abbey's book *Desert Solitaire*.[1] Brandon loaned me the book as a prerequisite read before Pat, Brandon, and I launched on a cross-country excursion to Moab, Utah and Canyonlands National Park, seven years before our trip to Death Valley. Abbey's poetic prose of buttes, mesas, pinon and juniper forests, arroyos, slot canyons, arches, and red sandstone rocks immediately hooked me. Pat and Brandon were both seasoned desert enthusiasts, Pat living and playing in Utah for many years and Brandon making numerous cross-country trips to the arid wildernesses of Utah, Arizona, New Mexico, and California. My first excursion to Utah left me yearning for more. I was more than ready to launch into a new desert destination.

---

1. Abbey, *Desert Solitaire*.

Seven years after that first epic arid adventure to Utah, I was eager to return to the desert and lands Edward Abbey spoke of with such eloquence. For this next desert trip, this time to Death Valley, our car rental of choice was an all-wheel-drive Nissan Pathfinder, which fit the four of us comfortably with all our camping gear. This time Kevin joined our travel ranks. We arrived on the outskirts of Death Valley National Park and its barren moonscape, and ultimately Badwater Basin, our first destination. Brandon was at the wheel; his driving speed, at seventy miles per hour, was only exceeded by his unbounded enthusiasm for this beautiful yet desolate landscape. Brandon was beyond excited to introduce one of his favorite lawless places on Earth to his three buddies. We blared U2's "Where the Streets Have No Name" with the windows rolled down, allowing the arid breeze and seemingly endless blue skies to embrace us all. We hastily parked the car and ran shirtless like little kids playing in the largest sandbox we ever saw, tossing our baseball caps into the stiff warm wind and watching them launch hundreds of feet down the flats.

Death Valley National Park backed up against the Nevada border to the east, and the 200,000-acre Inyo Mountains Wilderness to the west, and just beyond those peaks the vast and majestic Sierra Nevada mountain range. The "rain shadow" effect of the Sierra Nevada results in Death Valley being one of the driest places in North America. The national park comprises nearly 3.5 million acres, the largest in the continental US, the vast majority of which is classified as wilderness. Colorful park location names include the Funeral Mountains, Devil's Cornfield, Last Chance Mountain, Sidewinder Canyon, Desolation Canyon, and Telescope Peak. This would be our wilderness playground for ten days.

In addition to its natural history, Death Valley is equally

rich in its cultural history and plays host to some infamous tales. Its earliest people were the Timbisha Shoshone Native Americans living there for centuries prior to white settlement. Some Japanese Americans were incarcerated and interned in a Death Valley relocation camp during World War II. Charles Manson and his cult following briefly lived in Death Valley, staying at the notorious Barker Ranch in the late 1960s. We hiked and played among these rich historical remnants and artifacts, and the spirits of the souls who may have lingered.

We hiked the Ubehebe Crater loop and then headed to the Death Valley National Park visitor center and sat down at a picnic table. A family of four was sitting nearby, parents and children glued to their cell phones while surrounded by extraordinary scenery all around them. We exchanged silent looks and shook our heads in dismay. Edward Abbey described the sight of national park infrastructure and the paving of natural places to accommodate the throngs of sightseers as "industrial tourism." I couldn't agree more.

As much as we were hypnotized by the cultural and natural beauty of Death Valley along the beaten path closer to the tourist center, we all felt the strong pull to remove ourselves from humankind, at least the tourist type of humankind.

Brandon asked, "Does anyone want to come to town with me to get the tire fixed?" There was an awkward silence for several seconds. "I'm in!" I said. Pat and Kevin opted to sit in their camp chairs at the base of the Eureka Dunes and sip the remnants of our coffee supply, rest, and savor the landscape. The closest town was Big Pine, California, nearly seventy miles each way. The trip out to run this errand—fixing the tire and resupplying some critical beverages like coffee and beer—would involve driving across some of the most brutal desert in the country, climbing a mountain pass, and descending to the valley bottom to Big Pine.

Brandon and I set out north and then west from our campsite at Eureka Dunes, riding on our spare tire doughnut in the Pathfinder rental. Our tire had become a victim of the bony road and jagged rocks on the pass into the Dunes. We had our fingers crossed we wouldn't hit any sharp rocks, a frequent occurrence in this park. We were already violating several rental car rules by taking our car to Death Valley, and we would test the Pathfinder's abilities to the extreme in the coming days. We both felt a sense of liberation as we headed into the unknown landscape, crossing over the Inyo Mountains divide and its tree-less snow-covered mountaintop beauty and descending into the valley below. Goosebumps dotted my forearms at the first sight of the quaint town of Big Pine in the distance, embraced by the all-surrounding Sierra Nevada mountains abruptly rising from the valley flats, making the Inyo Mountains seem like foothills. It was raw and majestic at the same time. It felt inviting. I thought, "I could live here."

We found a car repair shop with friendly mechanics to plug our flat tire and engaged in some small talk. They seemed curious about our stay in Death Valley. We were anxious to pick their brains about a mythical desolate valley south of the Eureka Dunes called Saline Valley. Brandon felt pulled to the large hole in this three-million-plus-acre park, with no tourist amenities noted. He was intrigued by both its size and what the map did not show, the unknown that could await us. It was said to be accessible only by unmaintained desert roads, one from the north, one from the south, and one coming from Eureka Dunes. The road from the north was closed because of snow this time of year. Most visitors would be arriving from the south road. On our map, Steele Pass Road looked like the most direct route for us to take, at least as the crow flies.

When we asked the mechanics about this mysterious and legendary place, they both smirked and asked, "Oh, you mean the springs where the naked hippies hang out with the rattlesnakes?" Brandon and I exchanged glances, our interest piqued. This was the birth of our Zen travel guidance that directed us for the remainder of the trip. A divine directive had been bestowed upon us, albeit an oblique one.

Since we had some time to kill as the flat was being repaired, we drove through downtown Big Pine and passed by an inviting diner. Brandon and I felt the pangs of hunger luring us into the parking lot filled with pickup trucks. It was an old-school diner, 1960s vintage, featuring a large counter with sunshine-orange swivel stools, and ringed by booths with locals chatting it up over coffee. We were greeted by a smiling waitress. We both love the home-cooked and affordable meals that diners generally offer. We grabbed some seats at the counter and ordered up hearty omelets filled with cheese, sausage, and veggies, with sides of toast and home fries. Just what the doctor ordered after camping out in the wilderness for days. We asked our waitress about the Saline Valley rumors and the fabled naked hippies. She confirmed that she had heard stories similar to those our smirking mechanics shared, although from what we could gather, none of the Big Pine locals had experienced it themselves. The local residents seemed a bit intimidated by the rumors of hard-to-reach lands inhabited by LA hippies and held no interest in them. The mysterious hot springs information was all secondhand, from folks passing by.

Next, we hit the small local supermarket for our needed supplies. Since we still had some time to kill, we drove the rural roads just outside the village to get a sense of the landscape. It felt like we were in the middle of a Western movie set, with barbed-wire fencing and horses and cows grazing on the sparsely vegetated range. We drove back to the car repair shop where the mechanics swapped out the spare with the newly plugged tire, and we were on our way. We were both flying high, satiated from our comforting diner breakfast, resupplied with beer and coffee, and having the assurance of at least one spare tire in case we ran into trouble. We successfully completed our to-do list but also something else, something intangible. Brandon and I felt like something in us both had begun to shift on the inside as we embarked on becoming one with our surroundings, and ourselves.

Jim "Going Over the Inyo," part 2 (photo credit Brandon Dennis)

After pausing beside the dirt road and having my "Going Over the Inyo" moment atop the rental car hood on the way from Big Pine town back to our campsite, I climbed down to join Brandon in the car. Our enthusiasm was still roaring as we transitioned the Ryan Adams CD to U2's underappreciated *Pop* album. *Pop* was another of our favorite albums that I had introduced to Brandon several years prior. This album helped me overcome an emotionally devastating breakup ending a thirteen-year relationship with my ex, Lydia. Both of our consciousnesses shifted on the drive back to our campsite from Big Pine. We were fully present with our setting, each other, and ourselves. Time stood still, as we played our favorite songs on the album: the techno "MoFo," the bass-driven "If God Would Send His Angels," the searing guitar of "Gone," the romantically crushing "If You Wear that Velvet Dress," and the final two songs "Please" and "Wake Up Dead Man." The latter song was our mantra about those around us living life in a self-induced trance, not being fully present in the moment, like that phone-obsessed family back at the visitor center, not doing what Brandon and I were doing in *that* moment.

On our drive back to our friends at the Eureka Dunes site, Brandon and I began to imagine scenes of hot springs, hippies, and rattlers that those locals in Big Pine joked about and the mystic lore of that place and its people. We were at an important decision crossroads for the next and last phase of our trip. We previously had some group discussions about where we would head after our planned portion of our trip, but no final decisions had yet been made. We intentionally left time in our itinerary for unplanned activities, to be open to possibilities so we wouldn't be locked in. We wanted the freedom to pivot, based on what we were seeing on the ground and on what we were feeling in the moment. Some of our options included hiking in the nearby Sierra Nevada mountains or perhaps checking out Joshua Tree National Park which was relatively close by. But Brandon and I were thoroughly enticed by the hot springs' lore. We agreed we would tempt Pat and Kevin.

We later came up with a phrase for that first leg of our stay in Death Valley National Park—"Death," the tourist zone of the park. For the second leg of the trip, we wanted to bypass the trappings of Death Valley's more popular sites and get into the backcountry areas and more remote sections within the park, which we dubbed "Deeper Death." We camped in some of the wilder parts and unofficial camping areas, or as we like to say, "bootleg camped," near the Natural Bridge trail and the Eureka Dunes. The potential excursion into Saline Valley would mean journeying into the complete unknown, going to where we described as "Deepest Death." If we could convince Pat and Kevin, we would transition from "Death," to "Deeper Death," to "Deepest Death." Our descriptions of the "death" categories started as a rather obvious joke as we progressed into the various landscapes of this national park with that very name. But later these phrases began to be associated with us going deeper within ourselves. It is said people may feel most alive when closest to death. As the U2 song title suggested, "Wake Up Dead Men." Awake we would become, indeed.

Brandon and I screamed back into camp driving the SUV at a reckless speed, hooting out the windows as Pat and Kevin jumped to their feet. Our blaring encore of U2's *Pop* album was designed to entice the boys to our level of excitement. Kevin and Pat were stilled like statues by this spectacle as we blew past camp only to turn around and audio assault them once again, in juvenile fashion, from the other direction. This time, the boys turned the tables on us, shed their clothes, and began dancing around the campsite naked as we pulled in. Brandon parked the car, and I tossed them a bag of coffee that quickly turned into a football for an impromptu game of catch. It was a glorious welcome as we shared our Big Pine town tale and spoke in glowing tones about adventures that might be ours in the Saline Valley hot springs. It took some convincing, but Pat and Kevin agreed we should attempt the journey through Steele Pass and the glory awaiting on the other side, "Deepest Death."

We packed up camp, loaded our gear, and began our next adventure. Before Pat took the wheel, he shared an experience he'd had alone in the dunes. He described a one-on-one encounter with a desert beetle. After a week or so of travelling in this beautiful and rugged desert landscape, he was finally able to let go of the burden of work stress. Pat said he was at peace when he got down on his belly to watch a large desert beetle crawling along the sand and then stop to bask in the heat. He lay within inches of the beetle, gazing at it for nearly half an hour, fully present, as he cleared his mind and was then able to contemplate his future. I started noticing a pattern after my own post-Big Pine, "Going Over the Inyo" moment and now Pat sharing his experience with the beetle. The "moment," some kind of initiating event—however small—was needed for us individually to stop, cleanse the brain, and reset, followed by deep contemplation, and finally, epiphany.

Although the distance, as the crow flies, from Eureka to Saline Valley Hot Springs was relatively short, the road could better be described as a goat path. After a few uneventful miles, we slowed to a crawl and realized that one of us needed to walk in front of the car to direct the driver; the three of us took turns warning our driver Pat with hand signals, expressive faces, and sometimes frantic voices of all the obstacles and pitfalls that posed danger to us. There were only inches to spare side to side among the narrow canyon walls; we later labeled this "the birth canal." Many threats lurked below, threatening to smash the car's oil pan, as large random boulders lay strewn along the road. Those few dozen miles took nearly five hours to complete. Pat was focused and determined to make it through. It was here that Pat earned his trip nickname, Steele Pass Pat.

Since we approached Steele Pass from the less-traveled north, we encountered the most remote and undeveloped set of hot springs first. We had the springs to ourselves, or so we thought. We set up a campsite nearby. Pat and I opted to go for a short hike down to the next set of hot springs to explore, while Brandon and Kevin hiked a small nearby mountain. Pat and I discovered the lush greenery of the more developed hot springs just a short walk beyond the undeveloped hot springs, the welcoming inhabitants inviting us to come back later. We were eager to share our discoveries with the boys. On the way to our campsite, Pat and I encountered an almost ghostlike being walking in the desert. A woman wrapped entirely in white cloth from head to toe appeared. My mind conjured a female version of Peter O'Toole's character in the movie *Lawrence of Arabia*. We approached the stranger to initiate a conversation with her. She wanted no part of us, completely ignored us and headed off in the opposite direction. Pat and I looked at each other as if to say "WTF!" As she headed back to her nearby campsite, we noticed that tucked in the back of her white flowing garment was a foot-long knife. We rejoined Kevin and Brandon at our campsite and shared our story of the hot springs and of the bizarre encounter with the strange woman we met along the way.

The four of us explored the undeveloped hot springs near

our campsite. There were two small pools, less than ten feet long each and three feet deep, surrounded by overhanging desert grass and shrubs. We slid into the welcoming waters for a soothing soak, our bodies beginning to relax after the nail-biting trip. Pat and Kevin decided to leave the hot springs and head back to camp to eat dinner, while Brandon and I remained, sipping beer.

As the sun began setting, we were joined by uninvited guests arriving by air. Bats began to descend upon us as we soaked. They came in batches, plunging in to get a drink from the natural pool and to dine upon the insects hovering above the water. I wasted no time evacuating the springs, surrendering it to our winged friends. After soaking solo a little longer, Brandon also removed himself from the water but stood at its edge in awe of the spectacle. I watched from a safer distance away, afraid of contracting rabies. As the bats swooped in from the sky to the springs, they narrowly missed Brandon's body as he stood still. He then opened his arms in a cross-like fashion, almost inviting the bats to swirl around him. He was under the impression that the bats' internal radar would prevent any collisions with him. One bat crashed into his body, as Brandon remained still, albeit surprised. He appeared calm, his arms outstretched; bats flew by, narrowly avoiding him.

The white-clad stranger Pat and I had met earlier in the day entered the fenced hot spring area and paused to watch Brandon and the bats from afar without Brandon noticing her. A fascinated look filled her previously unemotional face. She approached him with a towel draped over her arm, and the two began to talk.

(Photo credit Brandon Dennis)

Brandon later shared that he tried to engage her in a nuanced conversation, given the story that Pat and I shared about her. She began to let her guard down ever so slightly, and kindly asked Brandon if he was done soaking, so that she could be alone in the hot springs. Near the end of their conversation, Brandon asked what her name was. She replied, "My name? You can call me—go fuck yourself." Brandon burst out laughing. It was that moment where he thought he cemented his relationship with this strange woman. Brandon grabbed his towel and left, and his ghostlike friend jumped into the hot springs to enjoy her solitary soak.

Brandon and I headed back to our campsite; he shared more of the story of his bat encounter and of the woman camping close by. We further debriefed about the surreal experience as we pounded the remaining beers in our cooler. We opted to abandon our tents and sleep under the stars. Brandon was awakened by a big white dog licking his face. It was the odd woman's dog. She walked over to our campsite to retrieve her pet. She had warmed to Brandon and invited him to see her campsite, and he later shared the experience with us. The back of her old-school Ford Bronco served as her sleeping quarters, while an array of colorful sheets, offering her some privacy, served as her living area. She shared her less offensive name with Brandon, Jayananda. She had spent summers in the Sierra Nevada mountains, camping out and going for therapeutic plunges in the various mountain hot springs there, returning to the desert hot springs in wintertime. She was on state disability due to a negative vaccination reaction. The hot springs contained high concentrations of lithium and other beneficial minerals. It almost felt to us like she was running from something or someone, or trying to find something, going deeper into herself. She had an outlaw aura about her, with her dog and her oversized knife affording her some sort of protection.

Jayananda walked over to our campsite after hosting Brandon at her own site. She became more at ease and began to trust our entire group, especially after Brandon's bizarre bat experience. Jayananda shared with us her seasonal hot-springs-therapy traveling schedules. She and Kevin began talking about their daily meditation rituals. Pat, Brandon, and I expressed our desire to learn how to meditate, since we had always found it difficult. Jayananda offered to lead us in a group meditation session. We sat with our legs crossed in a circle on the warm desert sands. She began by having us concentrate on our breath, a deep breath in, hold the breath for a few seconds, followed by an extended lung-emptying exhale. She then had us focus on our third eye, the energy chakra located in the middle of our foreheads, to channel the Universe's energy from above us and then through us. The third eye was the center of our intuition. She asked us to visualize the energy coming in through this chakra as a wispy white cloud. The group meditation reaffirmed our collective presence within this unique landscape, setting the stage for personal transformations yet to come.

She broke camp and departed later that day, while Brandon snapped a photo of her from a distance, without her knowing. We needed the photo as proof to assure ourselves that she was in fact real and not a desert mirage. When Brandon developed the photo, it simply showed a blurred, amorphous image, further adding to her mystical allure. Was she real? Did that really happen? Jayananda was our first surprise of the many more to come on this leg of our trip into the unknown. Brandon decided to grant the intriguing stranger a new title, "Saline, Goddess Warrior of Saline Valley." She and the desert valley we were currently inhabiting would be one and the same to us, as she exemplified this mysterious place full of surprises. Saline had become the desert, and the desert had become her.

We once again packed up our campsite and continued south on Steele Pass Road. After a short drive we arrived at the more developed lower hot spring. These springs were larger and surrounded by tall palm trees, creosote bush, desert holly, mesquite, and seemingly out-of-place manicured lush green lawn. The springs themselves were built of desert rock concrete, and their temperatures were regulated by underground pipes, so the water was not too hot. We were welcomed by one of the hot springs' regulars, Brad, who was sitting in a camp chair on the putting-green-like lawn, playing his guitar and singing, buck naked!

Our hot springs host, Brad, introduced us to his good buddy, Jeff. They were both shocked and deeply impressed when they learned we had arrived at their hot springs from

Steele Pass. It was extremely rare for visitors to come by that route. The narrow, boulder-strewn "road" was prone to flash flooding, even in this desert environment, causing road washouts. Steele Pass was the more fraught of the three possible roads in, and our choice earned us a hero's welcome.

Brad and Jeff insisted we stay overnight. They told us not to worry about food or beverages, at least for another day. We had not planned on camping at these hot springs. We intended to only spend the day relaxing before continuing south. Despite our stop in Big Pine a couple of days prior, we were once again running low on food, and more importantly, beer. Brandon and I put a hurting on our beer supply on our way back from Big Pine and after our bizarre encounter with Saline and the bats. Brad and Jeff began pulling out cheese, bread, smoked sausage, and beer to share with us. They just spread the food on a folding table with no plates, utensils, or napkins. Kevin, Pat, Brandon, and I looked at each other and decided we could not decline this gracious offer to spend more time in this melding of a natural and man-made desert oasis.

After our barbarian buffet, Brandon mysteriously retreated to his tent, while Pat, Kevin, and I were invited into the hot springs. This time our new friends and their camping neighbors soaked in the nude and invited us to do the same. It was just how things were done here. It was a co-ed soak, but not in any way sexual. So, the rumors from the mechanics and our waitress in Big Pine were true—naked hippies.

After our relaxing dip, we and our hosts dried off, got dressed, and walked over to a fire circle constructed with large boulders surrounded by benches as the sun began to set. We were introduced to Popcorn Bob as he made several batches of popcorn, popped over the open campfire. It was the most deliciously seasoned popcorn we ever tasted, and we told him as much, both sweet and savory at the same time. In a confidential aside, Popcorn Bob told us he made gourmet popcorn that he sold at music festivals across California. As he passed the popcorn around the circle, Brad started strumming his guitar and singing. Brandon quietly rejoined our group at the fire circle from his sequestered time in the tent.

Kevin, who was the only professional musician among our group, joined in with the singing. It was then that Kevin was awarded his trip nickname Desert Fox, since we fondly recalled hearing desert foxes serenading us throughout the trip. We also teased Kevin about his physical fitness and lean physique, also fox-like.

When Brad asked if we had any musical requests, the four of us blurted in unison, "U2, please." The *Joshua Tree* album had become the featured soundtrack of this desert trip. Our request resonated with these hot springs regulars; after all, Joshua Tree National Park was only a short drive from Death Valley. Brad launched into one of the more obscure songs on the album, but one of our favorites, "Running to Stand Still." I grabbed an empty five-gallon bucket, turned it upside down, and began playing percussion in tom-tom fashion, and we all joined in on the singing, with our group of four providing harmony. It was a magical moment under the starlit desert sky with an enormous crackling bonfire, among our newfound friends.

We soaked in the hot springs once again the following morning with Brad and Jeff. Pat served coffee to the group as we bathed, all in the nude again, including Pat. As we packed up and moved on, we said goodbye to the hot springs community, and they encouraged us to come visit again. Our hosts invited us to their annual nude softball game on Presidents' Day weekend, pitting two different hot springs communities against each other. That visual lingered in my mind.

Steele Pass Pat (on top), Kevin—the Desert Fox, and Jim —Big Pine (photo credit Brandon Dennis)

We continued heading south from the hot springs, stumbling upon an abandoned historic salt mine along the way. We learned from the national park signage that immigrant Chinese workers built mining roads to accommodate the booms of silver, gold, lead, quartz, borax, and salt forming the dozen towns which once housed hundreds and thousands of miners, bankers, store owners, prostitutes, and outlaws. When the booms were over, the towns were abandoned and all that remained were the ghost town and mining infrastructure, like tramways and remnants of storefronts.

We all felt the need to stop at the abandoned mine and process what had occurred in Saline Valley and express our gratitude before we left Death Valley. Brandon shared with us why he was squirrelled away in his tent the afternoon before.

21

As we sat at the outskirts of the deserted mine, he shared with us a sequence of events that happened while he was alone. Like Pat, Brandon had his own one-on-one encounter with a desert creature inspiring his time of awakening, his "moment." Brandon shared the story of what happened to him on the chilly early morning walk to find an appropriate spot to answer nature's call at our campsite near the undeveloped hot springs.

Big Pine, Diamondback, and Steele Pass at the
abandoned salt mine (photo credit Kevin Greenblott)

It was earlier on the same day as his encounter with the bats and Jayananda. A powerful thought blared in his mind, "Snake!" After he heard this voice, he looked down and stopped. A rattlesnake lay there curled up in front of him, camouflaged, blending in with rocks. The warning voice of the snake was speaking to him directly. Brandon heeded the warning and avoided the snake just in time. He described this fortunate forewarning as a switch that changed his conscious-ness. Everything felt different, surreal, and otherworldly. It felt like he'd walked through a portal and Saline Valley was like a parallel universe. It was this psychic happening that earned him his trip nickname, Diamondback. The message from the rattlesnake allowed his subsequent revelations to follow.

Here, at the abandoned salt mine, he shared he was deeply inspired by the events that unfolded while we were in Saline Valley and by his mystical experience with Jayananda and his interpretation of her as a desert goddess. He had disappeared into his tent for nearly two hours and had written a poem he called "Saline." He said the poem poured right out of him all in one sitting. We all sat at the base of an eerie yet fittingly humorous towering metal sculpture of bats, evoking Brandon's encounter just before he met Saline. Brandon read his poem aloud:

Stretching my arms out I challenge the skills of winged ones.
Staring straight ahead I feel a blur of motion.
I find myself at peace with a truce I have declined with fear.

Behind me I can hear the West walking around me watching.
With friends she approaches me open to the moment.
Our eyes engage and our words test each other.
Sentence by sentence we move delicately toward each other.

In awe and wonder I try and communicate with the mythical.
With fearlessness I convey the honesty of this journey.
Openly we dance around each other with the trust of children.
Tonight, we are playmates in the moment.

The beauty I walk upon is a woman.
In Death she has taken on a human form.
Sometimes I speak to her like I am speaking to the desert itself.
Skirting around the fringes of madness we break the connection
of sanity.
In Deeper Death there is an oasis to be found.

Diamondback
(excerpt from "Saline" by Brandon Dennis;
see A3 for full poem)

At the end of his reading, Brandon passionately described the significant influence he felt once we entered "Deepest Death." He was struck deep in his soul by the landscape and people we encountered and realized his epiphany. He shared with us an encounter he'd had in his youth when he met a stranger on a train in Colorado, named Kevin Palmer. That experience resonated with him again on this trip. In Kevin Palmer's long conversation with Brandon, he shared his life-long philosophy of not being burdened by the blinders of planning, being open to all possibilities, following signals and leads, and drifting into the unknown. Although he had dabbled in drifting before, Brandon's heeding of this stranger's guidance was fully realized two decades later on this trip. It would continue to hold sway on subsequent trips and adventures that followed for Brandon and me. It was the birth of what we now call "Zen Travel," or what had happened to us collectively, especially in the "Deepest Death" phase of the trip. Henceforth, Brandon would follow leads into the unknown, pay attention, and be open to the "guidance."

At different points along the trip, we were each struck by a shift in perspective, each coming away with new life epiphanies. Pat was about to become a dad for the first time, and he realized he needed to free himself from his stressful, toxic, and unfulfilling job so he could focus on his new family. He would be applying for a new job within the same company but doing more of what he loved. His fearless leadership in getting us through Steele Pass would give him the courage to make this job transition after the spark was lit in his "moment" with the beetle. Within four months after returning home from the trip, Pat changed jobs and became a dad.

Kevin, the Desert Fox, was motivated to take a year off from his carpentry job to focus on making a new album of his songs and trying to make a full-time living as a singer-songwriter. Kevin also decided to end the unhappy and unfulfilling dating cycle he was in. A few months after our trip he ended his relationship at the time. In the wake of this breakup, I encouraged Kevin to ask Trese out. They had met a few months before, and Kevin seemed smitten. Kevin and Trese started dating shortly thereafter, and the rest is history, as they are now happily married and have two daughters. Soon after the trip, he began work on his second album and fully focused on performing his music full-time.

My "moment" of deep bliss and affection for the tiny town of Big Pine cleared my everyday consciousness and allowed me to acknowledge how much I craved more presence and peace in my life. I confirmed my pre-trip inclination that I needed to end my unhappy and ever-confrontational marriage but do so in an amicable way. When I arrived home, I asked my then wife, let's call her "Sarah," to go for a walk in the woods. As gently as possible, I expressed, "I can't do this any longer." And, surprisingly, she agreed. We separated immediately and calmly. I felt completely unburdened and relieved, despite marital failure.

A few months after the trip, I proclaimed to myself and my close friends that this summer would be my "summer of infinite possibilities." I would be open, in Zen fashion, to whatever options might unfold. I would drift without plans, not necessarily in traveling, but in how I approached my life in each moment. I attended music festivals and concerts with my friends, camped, paddled, hiked, and dated in an unserious fashion, with full disclosure of my disinterest in commitment to my then partners. In August of that year, 2008, the height of that summer's events, the "infinity proclamation" was reaffirmed. In astrology circles, 08-08 is a symbol of infinity and carries with it profound spiritual significance. It can represent new beginnings and infinite potential.

(Photo credit Brandon Dennis)

That summer, and particularly the month of August, was the zenith of my personal freedom. I fully basked in the glory of late summer warmth, roaming unconstrained and unburdened. It was as if my "Going Over the Inyo" moment of bliss and consciousness shift on the hood of the rental car on the way back from Big Pine lingered with me like an aura. I was finally liberated and in my happy place.

The abandoned-salt-mine pit stop ended with the four of us expressing our gratitude to the Universe, to the life-changing events and motivations that engulfed us individually and collectively. We sprinkled our tobacco offering of gratitude to each other and to the goddesses of the North, South, East, and West. We jumped back in the car and headed west. We would day hike at the base of Mount Whitney in the Sierra Nevada on our way to our last destination, a cleansing plunge into the Pacific Ocean. Before heading back home, each of us carried a new life plan in our pockets, one that would be set in motion in the days and weeks ahead, all thanks to our "moments" under the umbrella of Saline Skies.

Saline Skies

© Jim Ryan and Lizzy Mandell

Over Steele Pass to Saline Skies
The springs are hot and the people kind
I wasn't sure what I might find
I went there to find some peace of mind
I went there to find some piece of mind

Rattlers and beetles cross the dune
Desert fox he sings his tune
Sleeping under stars and moon
Don't want to leave here anytime soon
I don't want to leave here anytime soon

Chorus
Two hundred feet beneath the sea
Enlightenment by epiphany
Nowhere else I'd rather be
The place they call Death Valley
The place they call Death Valley

Down the Inyos to Big Pine town
Sierras embrace and all surround
The diner where folks all gather around
Those who were lost they are now found
I was lost and now I'm found

Repeat chorus

Over Steele Pass to Saline Skies
The springs are hot and the people kind
I wasn't sure what I might find
I went to find some peace of mind
I just went to find some peace of mind

Scan the QR code to listen to the song,
performed by Lizzy Mandell

St. Patrick's Day, 2002

New York City

My head was reeling as I sat, stunned, in my driveway, listening to the Vermont Public Radio news coverage. It was the morning of September 11, 2001. Sitting in the car next to mine was Anita, a real estate appraiser. We both left our radios on as we got out, asking each other, "Are you listening to this?" "Who would do such a thing—and why?" In a single moment, our priorities had shifted. Anita had a full day of appraisals ahead of her, and my workday was booked with meetings I had to get back to. "Should we go ahead with the appraisal?" We decided she should complete her work to meet the bank's refinancing closing date. We walked quickly through my house. Perhaps we both needed to establish some sort of semblance of normalcy in the face of the absurdity of a mundane real estate transaction while our world and everything around us was coming undone? Since I didn't own a TV, I turned on the radio in my kitchen so we could both continue to listen. Our ears were glued to the ongoing coverage. On this morning, the entire world would change.

September 11 now remains seared in our collective memory. Most recall where they were when the planes hit the towers on that eventful day, as my parents' generation remembered exactly where they were when JFK was assassinated, and my grandparents' generation during the Japanese surprise attack on Pearl Harbor.

On the way from my office to my house for my house appraisal appointment that morning, I switched on Vermont Public Radio as I did most mornings, catching up on local, national, and international news. The regularly scheduled BBC program was interrupted with live reporting of a plane hitting one of the Twin Towers.

The normally objective and professional radio personalities stammered and paused for several seconds trying to discern what was unfolding and gather themselves. I leaned in, closer to my radio, to be nearer to the voices sharing the events unfolding across the airwaves. The reporters were focused on the people in the burning tower, as fire, police, and EMTs headed up the stairs, trying to rescue the thousands of workers in the building. The reporting was interrupted once again, this time to share that a second plane hit the second Twin Tower. The initial assumption was that the first plane hitting the tower was some sort of accident. When the second plane hit, the spec-ulation turned to a possible terrorist strike. Within minutes, the news was interrupted again with information about a third and fourth suspicious plane crash on the Pentagon building in Washington, DC, and in a field in western Pennsylvania, respectively. Then came the surreal scenes of people jumping out of the Twin Towers' windows. I despaired at the hopelessness compelling such desperate acts. All these terrifying events unfolded in the span of my short drive home. I felt my heart racing and my head spinning as I wondered if any of my family or friends happened to be in New York City that morning, a relatively short drive or train ride from their homes on Long Island.

One image that was continually running in my brain was of the New York City fire, rescue, and police personnel heading up the towers' stairs as thousands were desperately fleeing down those same stairs in the frantic minutes before the first tower collapsed. These first responders were still heading up the stairs in the second tower, even after the first tower collapsed. I remember listening to the coverage, trying to fathom how many thousands of workers and hundreds of responders might be trapped in the rubble, and how many would likely perish. The courage, valor, and selflessness from the fire, police, and rescue and recovery teams were unprecedented.

Thousands of fire department, police department, rescue squad members, and union workers spent weeks at Ground Zero, first attempting to find survivors and then to secure remains. Later we would learn that those same volunteers were putting themselves at risk, damaging their lungs from the toxic dust of the building rubble. My brother Chris, who was a Nassau County, New York, police officer at the time, commuted to the former Twin Towers site the day after the attack and for a week thereafter from Long Island to help in the recovery efforts. He wasn't required to be there, but he said he had to be there. He described the scene as emotionally overwhelming and the physical work of the debris removal grueling.

My father and I would occasionally attend the New York City St. Patrick's Day parade. I attended several times when I was living in New York, and less frequently after I moved to Vermont in 1990, where I celebrated the day of the Irish there instead. It was an annual acknowledgement of our Irish and Scottish heritage. My father's great-grandparents came over to the States from Ireland and Scotland in the late 1800s, first settling in the New York City area, with one branch of the family tree finding home in Digby, Nova Scotia. My dad made the pilgrimage to Vermont on several occasions, but that year, 2002, I brought my then girlfriend down from Vermont to attend the parade with me and my father. I felt deeply compelled to attend the parade in the city.

It was only six months since September 11' and emotions were still running high. In March of 2002, the world was still empathetic to the US and its citizens. Even some of our enemies, like Iran, conveyed their deepest sympathies to us, and meant it. On St. Patrick's Day 2002, New York City would be hosting the world, literally. More than three hundred thousand marchers came from around the world to show their support for the fallen police, fire, and rescue workers. Three million people attended the parade, including the president of Ireland, a first. Pipe-bands from Ireland, from both the Republic and Northern Ireland, and England marched side by side. Given their deeply tarnished history and decades of "the Troubles," this was unheard of. This sight was one of several that brought me to tears on this emotional day. Another one of those moments occurred when all three hundred thousand marchers paused midway through the parade, quieted their instruments, and faced the direction of the former Twin Towers location in a stirring act of tribute to those who fell on that day. Those two silent minutes felt like twenty.

The St. Patrick's Day Parade in New York City is normally a wildly festive affair. Spectators dress in their best Irish green attire, over-the-top party hats, T-shirts offering kisses to the Irish, shamrocks painted on faces, and alcohol flowing freely, starting in the early morning hours at the parade's onset. On this day, the roistering revelry and debauchery were more reserved, at least during the somber ceremonies. Seas of green buffered the parade's edges. Many fire, police, and rescue department members carried photos of their deceased coworkers cradled in their arms or slipped into the bands on their uniformed hats. Other parade participants included local high school and university bands, labor union groups, various Emerald Societies, the Ancient Order of Hibernians, the city's Sanitation Department and Corrections Department, New York City's mayor, and New York State's governor and its US senators and representatives. It seemed like any organization of importance was in attendance on that day.

Many of the marching organizations carried their own banners and were accompanied by their own bands and floats. In the lead procession, marchers carried 343 individual flags, representing the fire, police, and EMT personnel who lost their lives on September 11. Many also held banners reading "343." Dozens of pipe-bands accompanied the marching organizations. Each piper's uniform included a Scottish handcrafted tartan kilt with box pleats, traditionally representing the clan or region of the wearer, a black wool cap, a white collared dress shirt, black silk tie, wide leather belt with a large buckle, thigh-high woolen hose with garters, black leather shoes, and sporran pouch, to hold keys and wallets, since kilts don't have pockets. Each band member wore their uniforms proudly with chests out and heads high, especially on this day of seminal ceremony.

As the marchers reached the end of the parade route at Seventy-Ninth Street near Central Park, they headed to the bars. Most of the parade participants wore black armbands, which contrasted starkly with the thousands of fervent fans in green-cladded costumes, green makeup, and shamrock sunglasses, ready to let their collective hair down and honor St. Patrick, the patron saint of Ireland and Irish heritage and culture. The emotional embrace of the parade carried over into the tightly packed bars near the parade route, especially the Irish bars. The pipes and drum bands, the other marchers, and parade attendees alike came from across the country and globe, and they were now drinking for their fallen brethren. The bartenders and waitstaff were overwhelmed as people dozens deep bellied up to the bars waving cash. Bar tables were filled with empty glasses, their surfaces covered with sticky residue of beverages carelessly spilled. The clinks of toasts to those lost and clanking glasses hitting the bar resounded in the room.

The release of emotion that day made the drinks go down especially smoothly for me. We drank with many police and firefighters from across the country and across the globe. My credit card came out often, as I bought drinks for many of the marchers and responders we connected with in those bars on that day. I proceeded to get shit-faced drunk—and later, ingloriously sick. My father matched me drink for drink, but he seemed to handle it a bit better than I did.

My girlfriend enjoyed being a relatively sober spectator for the day's activities and photo-documented the entire day. She framed a set of two photos of me and my dad. The "before" photo shows us just arriving at the parade, with Dad wearing his unicorn hat. Dad was known for wearing appropriately inappropriate headwear for special occasions. I opted for the more traditional red plaid woolen Irish driving cap. The "after" photo was of me the next day with Dad, looking like I was on the defeated end of a heavyweight boxing match, with swollen, half-open eyes, wearing a pained smile. These photos remain in my father's current apartment, and he loves to remind me of my less than stellar performance.

To some, bagpipes give the chills and stir deep haunting emotions of Celtic pride. To others, the bagpipes sound like a bird being strangled or like fingernails screeching along a chalkboard. I have always fallen into the former camp. On that sunny, chilly St. Patrick's Day, the dozens of parading pipebands provided me a day of goosebumps.

Shortly after attending this parade, I decided I needed more bagpipes in my life. I joined the Catamount Pipe Band in Vermont. I was not confident I could learn to play the complicated bagpipes, so instead I was drawn to the instrument I knew, or at least somewhat knew, the snare drum. I had been a frustrated desk and table banger my entire childhood and young adulthood. I would achieve my lifelong dream of being amongst the pipers, accompanying their plaintive drones and buoyed by the applause of cheering bystanders as I marched in parades, proudly wearing my tartan kilt and uniform with my Celtic brethren.

The world needed a place to gather, to grieve, and to celebrate those whose lives were lost on September 11. New York City on St. Patrick's Day, six months following that tragic day, was that place. It captured the shared sentiment all were feeling in that moment. My father and I needed to be there. The normally disparate several million in attendance and watching the live coverage converged in what felt like the grief, compassion, and empathy of one being.

St. Patrick's Day, 2002

© Jim Ryan and Joanne Breidenstein

Went to New York on St. Patrick's Day
To see waves of green on parade
Red fire trucks and police in dress blue
Marched for two miles down Fifth Avenue

Drones of bagpipes warmed the cold city air
Widows in black, blankly stared
Dublin and London marching side by side
Former foes now united by pride

Chorus
Paid their respects from around the world
"343" flags unfurled
Fresh in our minds, just six months through
St. Patrick's Day, 2002
St. Patrick's Day, 2002

Gathered in the bar across from Penn
Held glasses high to our fallen men
That ran up the towers as others fled
Names were spoken, tears were shed

Repeat chorus

Wish I Met You Sooner
Tavernes, Spain

The rowdy Irish headed for their charter bus after leaving the reception. No one wanted to have to drive back to the hotel after a night of drinking at the wedding. As I was about to get in Vin's rental car, I realized I had forgotten my suit jacket inside. I walked across the parking lot to retrieve my jacket, and brogue-tinged voices from the open windows shouted, "Jim we have your jacket. It's in the bus." The door opened, and I entered and walked up the stairs. Voices from the back of the bus stated, "Your jacket is here, in the back." As I proceeded to walk down the aisle, the door abruptly shut, and the bus started to pull out of the lot. My fellow passengers began to laugh in a devilish way. At that moment I realized I was being abducted. I walked over to an open window and shouted to Vin and his family, who were standing beside the rental car waiting for me, "I'll see you in the morning." They grinned and shook their heads. It was a consensual abduction.

Vin and I lived three houses down and across the road from each other on Pinedale Avenue in Farmingville, Long Island. We have been friends since we first met in kindergarten. I spent most of my early childhood through my junior year of high school in that house, until my father moved us away after my parents divorced.

Vin, his older sister Pacqui, and their parents were from Spain. Vin was born in Spain and lived there until his family moved to the US when he was two years old and Pacqui was ten. After Vin's parents died, he inherited an apartment there with a balcony overlooking the Mediterranean Sea. Vin asked me if I wanted to join him and his family for two weeks in Spain, where we would also attend the wedding of Pacqui's stepdaughter, Siobhan.

Paqui had moved to Ireland when she was in her thirties for a job there with an insurance agency. Paqui met an Irishman, a business owner and the mayor of a small town called Fermoy in County Cork in the southwest of the country. Her husband, Michael, had adult children from a previous marriage, including Siobhan. Siobhan would be marrying her long-time boyfriend, Jarif. Siobhan and Jarif would be bringing several dozen of their closest friends and family from Ireland to a destination wedding on the Mediterranean coast of Spain. And I had never been to Spain, nor met the bride and groom.

I am not a big fan of attending weddings. I worked too many as a restaurant and bar manager witnessing the same old ceremonies and unoriginal DJ playlists predominantly featuring the chicken dance and other cringeworthy, cheesy traditions, like the bride and groom smearing each other's faces with wedding cake. But this one would have the makings for something completely different and mysterious. Something inside me stirred. I knew I couldn't say no to this invitation.

The first week of our trip was dedicated to the Irish wedding. The crew from Ireland flew in a day after we arrived in Tavernes, located fifty miles south of Valencia. Tavernes de la Valldigna is a horseshoe-shaped valley bordered on the west by the Iberian Mountains and the Mediterranean on the east; sandwiched in between are the fertile and flat agricultural lands of orange groves, rice paddies, and olive trees. Our wedding contingent gathered daily for meals at local restaurants, most with outdoor dining rooms along the Mediterranean. We feasted on fresh fish, cheeses, paella, and tapas, Spain's version of appetizers, served with copious amounts of Spanish red wine. While the late afternoons and evenings were booked with wedding guest gatherings, our daytimes at the apartment were filled with playing in the sea. Vin's kids Brittany and Vincent and I enjoyed soaking in and riding the tranquil waves.

As the week progressed, my friendship with the contingent from Ireland grew. We gathered as a group every day leading up to the wedding. One evening, after the rest of the group went back to their rooms following a traditional late Spanish dinner, two of Siobhan's brothers and a handful of Irish friends and I decided to have a night on the town at a local disco. The brothers were drunk and danced all night long with big smiles on their faces, at one point dancing atop an elevated platform in 1960s go-go dancer fashion.

The disco's bouncer staff began to gather nearby, keeping an eye on Siobhan's brothers Colin and Justin. The dancing must have been the last straw, as several very burly Spanish bouncers wearing tight-fitting, short sleeve black polo shirts with their muscular arms bulging out, began escorting the two brothers out. A couple of bouncers turned into four, and now they were forcefully removing the pair. They began to rough them up for no apparent reason—my rowdy friends were not resisting their escorted exit. I intervened since I spoke passable Spanish, and both brothers did not speak any. I attempted to say, "please don't hurt them, they are nice guys and doing no harm." The group of bouncers completely ignored me. If anything, they became more violent in their removal efforts. I followed close behind, continuing with my pleas in broken Spanish. The bouncers then turned on me. The intoxicated brothers could only watch events unfold from the curb.

All four of them jumped on top of me, attempting to hold me down. One by one, I succeeded in throwing off all the bouncers who had me wrapped up, our fists swinging. There was an awkward pause in the action as I did a quick scan of my body to see if I was injured, to find that only my shirt was torn. Relieved, I stood straight up and smiled at the bouncers. They too seemed surprised at what had just unfolded, and one gave me a little smile back and another nodded at me. This kind of tussle must have been some sort of entertainment for them.

After the nightclub incident, I was treated like a hero by the pie-eyed lot. Back at the hotel they poured me drinks and cheered my name. The following day, they shared the story with the rest of the wedding party. And just like that, I became an honorary member of the Irish wedding group who until days ago were complete strangers.

I found it very easy to bond with Siobhan and her brothers, since they were only a few years younger than I was. We went out to the bars after our elaborate meals, when the older folks in the group went home to bed. At one of our outings, I found myself sitting alone with Siobhan at the bar. Siobhan was an executive director of an international food aid nonprofit. Her work entailed travel to many far-flung corners of the world, especially impoverished countries in Africa. I was fascinated by her travel stories. We dove into conversations about food sovereignty, my travels to Central America, and my strong desire to farm. We discovered we were local food advocates and geeks.

As we continued our conversation over pints at the bar, she gently touched my hand and suddenly, softly, stated, "I wish I met you sooner." I didn't quite know how to respond. "WTF!" first came to mind. I was taken aback by that strange statement, since we had only met a few days before, and she was about to get married in the coming days. While I was intrigued by her life's work and felt a connection there, I felt no romantic spark and it was not clear she was interested in me romantically, other than sharing her bizarre statement with me. I decided to let her hanging statement do just that, hang. I did not want to complicate our budding friendship, or her marriage for that matter. I later confided to my buddy Vin about Siobhan's pronouncement, and asked him, "What did she mean by that?" Vin gave me a sideways glance and half smile, as if to say, "What do you think it meant, you idiot?" Siobhan's statement lingered in my mind for the rest of the trip, and the following months and years.

After the wedding, when the bus was on the move, I sat down, and the happily buzzed passengers handed me my jacket and a bottle of Jameson Irish Whiskey, which was being passed from row to row. The entire busload of riders was singing passionately. The song enchanted me. Once I began to understand the words they were singing, I joined in. "No, nay, never, no nay never no more." I later learned that the song was "The Wild Rover," an anthem in Ireland. When I later asked some of my Irish friends about why they sang this song so passionately, I was told the original song is about an Irishman returning home after many years away, a homecoming of sorts. The narrator sings in his favorite hometown pub about his strong desire to stay rooted in the place where he grew up and end his wild roving days. To this day, that song brings me chills. I was deeply moved by the impact one song can have on an entire nation for much of its history. It was yet another surprise to me, as both a witness to and now participant in the unfurling circumstances being presented to me.

When the bus arrived back at the hotel on the Mediterranean, most of the passengers disembarked and adjourned to their rooms to collapse. Since I wasn't staying at the hotel and was without transportation, I wasn't sure what my Irish friends had in store for me. The newlywed couple told me they were headed up to their room to change out of their wedding clothes and would be right back down. Siobhan's brother Michael-David kept me company while we waited for them to return.

Siobhan and Jarif returned, now wearing comfortable clothes and carrying two bottles of champagne and some glasses. They said, "Let's go to the beach." The champagne was popped and consumed as hoots and congratulations were given. After Jarif downed a glass of champagne, he turned to his new bride and quietly said, "Honey, I'm going to bed," and gave her a little peck on the cheek. She gave him a kiss back and said, "Good night, love." I was stunned by his sudden departure, as it was their wedding night. Jarif seemed almost businesslike, especially on their most sacred day.

Now it was just me, Michael-David, and Siobhan. We opened the second bottle and consumed it in quick fashion. It was nearly dawn, as we watched the sun's illumination as it crested the horizon. Siobhan and her brother said goodnight to me, hugged me, and left for their hotel rooms.

Alone, shaking out the champagne cobwebs, and bemused by the events that occurred in the previous few days, I began walking down the beach in the general direction of Vin's apartment, which was several miles away. I stopped for a quick break and fell asleep on the sand. When I woke after a few hours, I continued along the remaining distance on the coastal sand back to Vin's apartment. Along the way, I pondered the unfolding events from the night before. It all felt very surreal. Who could imagine a woman about to become a bride uttering such a profound statement, "I wish I met you sooner," to someone she had just met, and then spending her wedding night on the beach with that same man and her brother, while her new husband went casually off to bed? As strange as it was, it brought a big grin to my face. It felt like I had been adopted by some dysfunctional Irish family and welcomed in to see their good, bad, and ugly on open display for me, all in the span of one week. It was one of the most fun and spontaneous weeks of my life.

I began to realize that the new, crazy, and passionate people I may meet from different cultures and perspectives, all await me when I say yes and remain open. When I reflect upon what occurred in one week, I am reminded of all the possibilities that await when I let go of any preconceived plans, when I take a swing and hit the curveball presented to me and remain open to what events might unfold. (See A.2 for a behind-the-scenes look at the creation of the fact-fiction hybrid song, influenced by this experience, that follows.)

Met You Sooner

© Jim Ryan and Dave Keller

Touched down, on the Emerald Isle
Cross the pond, Dublin skies
Headed south, along the Irish Sea
June wedding, 2003

Magdalene, oh, the bride to be
Drove from Galway, night before her big day
Let her long black hair, fall to her waist
We pulled back the stouts, and talked until late

Chorus
She smiled and said kind of slow
It's like I already knew you
We could have made quite a life, you know
Wish I'd met you sooner

After the vows, on the charter bus
I stumbled in with a bottle of Jameson
Wedding guests broke into song, sang the Wild
*   Rover*
Like I never heard before

Back at the hotel, bride and groom offered me a
*   glass*
They just poured, didn't even ask
He went to bed, we headed to the beach
Dark turned into day while we held each other's
*   hands*

Repeat chorus

When I'm at home, I've been known to drink
When the time is right
I'll drink a little of that Jameson
Late into midnight
I'll just close my eyes
And it's her that I see
And I'll fly away, fly away
To the Irish Sea

Alternative chorus
Oh Magdalene, Magdalene
It's like I already knew you
We could have made quite a life, you know
I wish I'd met you sooner

Scan the QR code to listen to the song,
performed by Dave Keller

Come Home to Me

Vermont and Negril, Jamaica

I had only been dating "Sarah" for a few months when, in a moment of romantic spontaneity, I suggested we climb up on my porch roof to catch the spectacular September sunset. A ladder was already in place, since the porch roof construction had just been completed. I had secretly carried up a bottle of champagne and two glasses in my daypack. Once on top, I popped the champagne and then popped the question. This otherwise rational and practical Capricorn went over the edge of irrationality and decided to propose. After a prolonged pause—she was clearly not prepared for this impromptu proposal—Sarah smiled broadly and said yes. After all, Sarah and I were both approaching forty years old. Her biological clock was more than ticking, it was thumping. We had no time to waste in getting married and attempting to get pregnant. It would likely be our last chance to procreate without artificial means, or at least *her* last chance. My strong desire to have children in my late thirties and early forties led to one of my most poorly thought out decisions: rushing to get married.

For most of my adult life I thought I would have children. I enjoy being Uncle Jim to my nieces and nephews and to a handful of my friends' kids. I treat them with respect and give them my full presence, like I would with adults. I believe in the saying "You will be judged by how you treat children and pets, when no one else is looking." I enjoy riding the surf, cannonballing with the kids, and playing hide-and-seek as much as the little ones do. I make it my practice to infuse humor when playing with kids and have been known for "scaring" children with my foam shark dorsal fin strapped to my back while swimming in lakes, sneaking up on unsuspecting young ones until we both laugh hysterically. I'm a big kid at heart and they seem to appreciate my somewhat dark sense of humor.

I had been partnered up in numerous long-term relationships where procreating was certainly possible. I engaged in conversations with various ex-girlfriends about having kids. But in each instance that dream was kiboshed when the relationship came to a screeching halt before the possibility of having children could be realized. In my long-term relationship with Lydia (described in the Transformation section), she spoke about the possibility of having a little "ham," as she liked to describe babies. Then that discussion was suddenly dropped like a hot potato, for no obvious reason. I was too busy being a fun-loving young adult to pursue the question of why she had a change of heart. I thought maybe she might change her mind in the years to come.

After my relationship with Lydia ended suddenly and before I met Sarah, I bought my first house and ninety acres in Washington, Vermont, affectionately called The Holler. One of the first things I did there was to go to the local animal shelter and pick out a shelter mutt, Alfred, or I should say he picked me out. I named him after Alfred Hitchcock, one of my favorite directors. After the rough breakup with Lydia, Alfred was my steadfast companion. Caring for him really helped me, but there was still something missing. I had this cozy two-bedroom place in the country with a pasture, a barn, some livestock, and chickens, and thought it might be time to share it with someone. I was not looking for a live-in girlfriend situation, but I was all alone and needed some company, especially after the tough breakup.

I heard an ad on the local radio station expressing the dire need for foster parents in Vermont. I turned off the radio and dialed the number without a second thought. The county youth services program was eager to welcome me on board as a foster parent. I would first have to pass their vetting process, background checks, and foster parent certification training. When meeting with a state social worker, I expressed the desire to ease my way into foster parenting, perhaps just stepping in a couple weekends a month. After all, I was a single guy working full-time and managing ninety acres of property. The social worker had other plans for me, and since I was a newbie to foster parenting, I lacked the self-confidence to say otherwise.

"Brian" lived in the same town and had just been removed from his family's home. The youth services agency wanted to keep him in the same school, if possible, and they thought I would be a perfect fit to provide Brian with a positive male role model. I initially resisted and then slowly warmed up to the idea. Brian lived with me for several months. He was a good kid, but with some very troubling behavioral issues. He had to be supervised by me at "arms distance" any time we were in public. I intentionally did not seek out the details about Brian's past. I did not want to judge him. I wanted to give him a clean slate, other than needing to know how to keep him and those around him safe. Within a few months, he was expelled from school, ran away, got into fights, caused scenes in public places, was caught smoking cigarettes and pot, and damaged my home. As a single parent working full-time, I was in over my head despite my best efforts. The situation was untenable, and Brian needed to be placed at a new home.

After Brian left, the youth services program wanted to assign me another full-time foster kid. This time I firmly declined but offered to be a part-time respite provider for other foster parents. I would be giving both the parents and kids a break from each other, generally for the weekend. My "specialty" was being the respite foster dad for teenaged boys.

For five years I hosted foster kids, providing weekends away for teenaged boys that were living at a nearby group home. Some weekends I would have two teens staying at my place at the same time. I offered the young men something different from the group home. I introduced them to nature and the outdoors. I took them canoeing and hiking. We went for long walks in my woods and roasted marshmallows around a campfire. I taught them some of the constellations I knew in the night sky. I showed them my favorite swimming holes and even set up a "drive-in movie" at home, placing the TV and DVD player outside on a starry night while we sat in camp chairs eating popcorn. I tried to teach them important life skills, like how to shop for groceries or manage money, or how to iron their shirts for job interviews. My parents divorced when I was thirteen years old, and my brothers Chris and Sean and I had to fend for ourselves more or less, often shopping and preparing our own meals and dividing up the household chores. I tried to imagine the kinds of help I would have welcomed back then and provided that to the boys I hosted.

My place in the country was not a good fit for all the kids. Some protested that I didn't have cable TV or good Wi-Fi, or that I limited their computer game time. But most of these young men enjoyed staying at my homestead and requested me personally for their respite weekend destination. Recently, I ran into one of those under my part-time care. I recognized him although he had grown up, was married, and had a young child of his own. He thanked me in front of his wife and infant daughter for taking such good care of him, showing him the outdoors, and treating him with respect. I felt like I made a difference for these otherwise untethered teens, and it gave me a strong sense of purpose.

Shortly into the marriage with Sarah, signs of marital strife began to surface, and in hindsight, there were red flags while we were engaged and even on the honeymoon. Despite our similar homesteading lifestyles and love of the outdoors, we discovered we were not well-suited for each other nor compatible in many other ways. It was the oil and water of personalities. In less than two years we both decided to end our marriage. For me, the moment of truth came on an epic camping adventure in Death Valley National Park (described in the "Saline Skies" essay), where the decision to divorce was hatched in a moment of deep presence and epiphany. I consider it fortunate that we did not conceive any children and did not have to put a child through a divorce or witness a very unhappy marriage.

After I moved to Bear Swamp from The Holler and my "person," Katie, moved in with me, she made it crystal clear that she did not want to have children. Early in our relationship Katie declared, in no uncertain terms, that she would not be giving birth. The thought of it made her physically ill. But she loved interacting with younger children from the ages of kindergarten up to middle school, her sweet spot age range, as part of her job working for a local nonprofit, managing a student truancy program. We are both considering stepping up to the emergency need for foster parents in Vermont; this time for us, it would be part-time respite care.

One January early morning while on vacation in Negril, Jamaica, an overpowering vision came to me in one of those half-asleep, half-awake moments. The vision rocked me awake. I was overcome with a strong sensation that maybe, just maybe, I could be a father and grandfather. It almost felt as though I was being sought out by someone.

Being awoken by the overpowering lucid dream got my mind churning. I quietly rolled out of bed. I made myself a cup of strong Blue Mountain Jamaican coffee and headed to the walkout patio in the predawn tropical darkness. A warm breeze caressed my face. I began scribbling down lines in my notebook about the newfound possibilities as I listened to the gentle surf rolling in and out only two hundred feet away. My writing and processing of the lucid dream later became the lyrics to the song "Come Home to Me." What if I already had a child out there? As a guy, it was certainly possible, despite my best efforts to use protection or at least verify my sexual partner was on birth control. I had fully explored both serious and not-so-serious relationships in my twenties and early thirties. But accidental pregnancies could happen even under the best of circumstances. Perhaps a partner opted not to tell me if such a thing occurred after we had parted ways?

With my stops and starts in wanting to have kids with different partners and then not, for various reasons, I now began envisioning myself as a grandparent. Becoming a parent seemed completely out of the question when I was in my late fifties. Most of my family and friends were either grandparents or would be becoming grandparents sometime soon. Being a grandparent seemed like a natural transition from my role as Uncle Jim and as a foster parent, enjoying the company of kids, but without the full-time commitment.

Around this time, programs like *Finding Your Roots* on PBS were taking off. My brother Chris began looking into our family history. He and our father had purchased the now readily available DNA kits and sent samples in. The murkiness of our family tree, on both sides of our family, was becoming clearer regarding what regions of the world my ancestors were from. But what if I had a son or daughter out there and they tried to find me?

It seemed like the Universe was trying to send me a signal that I could have fathered children unknowingly. I have always been intrigued by the mystical, and I visited with psychics and mediums on occasion. Three subsequent sessions with two different psychics and one shaman from Peru insisted that I had children, two, to be exact. But instead of feeling a sense of regret or dread, I thought it could be a positive development. I could have kids and potential grandkids out there. Maybe the psychics and shaman were correct? Still, raising kids involves the decision and lifelong commitment of two individuals in the relationship. I was only one of two votes, and not the final decision-maker. But that phone call or knock on my door would be my ultimate life curveball indeed.

Come Home to Me

© Jim Ryan and Dave Keller

Chorus
I know you're out there
I know you have to be
I can just feel it
Please come home to me

I never had my own family
I'm just here all alone
Hoping something good will come at last
From these seeds I may have sown

Those youthful indiscretions
Single days and one-night stands
I'd find you if I only could
Believe me I'm not a bad, bad man

Repeat chorus

Maybe you're a doctor
Are you flying rockets in the skies?
Maybe you're saving the world
Do you have my eyes?

I dream about you every night
It's come to consume me
I'd make a good grandfather for your kids
I can only hope it will be

Bridge
Until then, I'll wait for that phone call
Until then, I'll wait for that knock on my door
Until then, I'll be waiting for you

Repeat chorus

Scan the QR code to listen to the song,
performed by Dave Keller

SENSE OF PLACE

Judevine

Bear Swamp Farm, Vermont

I maneuvered down four rut-filled miles of muddy gravel road north of Wolcott Village, famous—or better, infamous—for Buck's Furniture's cluster of drab dark brown buildings. Each time I journeyed past the hill farm nestled above the large swamp complex to help my friend Nancy with her maple sugaring operation, I was struck by this place that seemed frozen in time.

For me, this place—now my farmstead—and its immediate surroundings, always looked inviting and intriguing. It was the early aughts when I asked Nancy who lived there. I wanted to know the farmers' story, how they had made their living and what their lives were like. Nancy said it was the Colgrove Farm, Frank and Eva's place. Frank had passed away in 2001 at the age of ninety-three, but Eva, then in her late eighties, was still living there on her own. Nancy and her ex-husband had befriended Frank and Eva and sugared on the land once owned by the mentoring couple. After Nancy's divorce, I helped her cut trees and limbs and shovel snow off the sugaring lines, repair downed lines, and tap trees on snowshoes. Inside the sugarhouse, we were bathed by an endless steam billow trying to escape through the siding gaps and cupola, while the caramel condensate clung to the metal roof and then dripped upon the heads of those inside. Work was often tedious and yet rewarding. Hours were spent feeding sugar wood to the hungry evaporator at regular intervals. Simultaneously, we checked sap levels, temperature, density, and apron sheeting, awaiting the magical moment when sap becomes syrup. At the end of the season, we cleaned the tubing lines. Eva and Frank's old-school bucket system with sap collected by draft horses was replaced with tubing lines, and a vacuum system and later with high-tech reverse osmosis. There is something to be said for keeping things as simple, and as quiet, as possible in the woods.

Frank and Eva Colgrove

For ten years, starting in the year 2000, I lived in Washington, Vermont, a half hour southeast of the capital, Montpelier. I bought a home and piece of land on Woodchuck Hollow Road, and my friends dubbed my homestead "The Holler." The Holler included ninety acres of mostly forest land, but I wanted a place with more farmland. I wanted to be a farmer, at least part-time anyway. Despite my connection to the land in The Holler, I grew discontented and ill at ease. The Holler was originally part of a several-hundred-acre dairy farm, which had been subdivided. At the time I bought my place, several suburban homes dotted the former farm. Many of these home-owners were obsessed with suburban lawn mowing and leaf blowing, disturbing my otherwise peaceful existence. I needed to find a new home, and I was looking for a farm, a farm located in a quiet and beautiful spot. Finding such a farm, within my price range, was a challenging proposition.

After trying unsuccessfully to buy a farm near Washington, my quest took a turn north, back to Lamoille County. I had spent several years renting there and working in the restaurants in nearby Stowe while I attended Johnson State College, now part of Vermont State University, and served as an AmeriCorps member, Bill Clinton's iteration of the Peace Corps. The Lamoille Valley was familiar territory for me. I remained close with many of my college friends and former colleagues amongst the restaurant and bar working class in Stowe. The Lamoille Valley was my hiking, paddling, camping, and live-music-attending playground. It felt like home.

A few years into my stint as Nancy's helper, I was driving by the old Colgrove place, and I noticed the hill farm looked uninhabited, and a new realtor sign adorned the front yard. I asked Nancy where Eva Colgrove was. She said Eva's daughters decided to move her to a nearby nursing home. The daughters were concerned after a chimney fire because Eva continued to run the woodstove. Eva wanted to stay at the farm, but her daughters decided the move was in Eva's best interest, both for her safety and their convenience. Although tinged with sorrow for Eva, this felt like an intervention from the Universe, discov-ering my dream farm—the homestead paradise that I admired for years—was now for sale.

It was love at first sight. I felt an instantaneous and deep connection to this land and its setting as I first sat at the top of the hill directly behind the house with a sweeping view of the property. The homestead was nestled in its own little valley, Judevine Mountain and The Ledges to the east looking down on the small farmhouse, which was surrounded by a large tamarack and speckled alder wetland. Balsam firs encircled the swamp, with red maples directly behind. Deeper within grew a mix of northern hardwood, spruce, and hemlock trees. The scene conveyed a bucolic and boreal feel at the same time. It was quite the juxtaposition—rugged ledge-exposed mountains, wild-looking swamp land, and an island of fertile farmland, prime agricultural soils. In Vermont, it's rare to see these habitat combinations in the same location. Best of all, no neighbors were within sight. It was quiet, other than all the sounds of nature in spring.

The farm and surrounding lands provided ideal feeding and cover habitat for waterfowl, deer, moose, mink, bear, beaver, songbirds, coyotes, fox, fisher cats, weasels, wood-chucks, porcupines, skunk, and raccoons. Many of these species would later provide unique challenges for our small farmstead. A half dozen one-hundred-year-old apple trees shaded the back yard, and at the end of the row of apple trees radiated the hallelujah crown of a bigtooth aspen and two larger-than-life balsam firs, which stood guard in the front horseshoe drive.

The landscape, I learned, was called Bear Swamp, or known by its fictional name, Judevine. The late David Budbill and his wife, Lois, lived in the next house up the road. Budbill, a well-respected author and poet, described Bear Swamp as "great and remote, wild and lonely," and declared the Colgrove Farm located in the southwest corner of the Northeast Kingdom as "one of the most beautiful places on earth."[1] I couldn't agree more. This landscape inspired many of David's plays, poems, and works of fiction as he wrote from his home office, looking out the window. The Budbills would later become good friends as well as neighbors.

I recall as a child trying to arrive at a place I would now call transcendence, when I wandered off in the woods behind my house to explore and sit for hours. When I was growing up, I was unaware of terms such as "mindfulness," "being present," or "meditation." I did not understand at the time why I needed my alone time, only that when I was able to bask in solitude, I felt so much better. My natural surroundings embraced and welcomed me. I often took off my shoes to feel the forest floor on my bare feet, grounding myself to it. I stared for long minutes at the treetops swaying in the light wind and the blue sky and felt the crisp air on my face. It seemed, even then, when I had my alone time in the forest, I could come back and face the world refreshed and in a better state of mind. Yes, I was truly an introvert, but it was more than that. An extroverted person needs companionship to recharge. Being alone was not only how I recharged, but it was also, and still is, a core part of my spirituality. The outdoors was my church, and I required regular worship. It was my first feeling of sense of place and connection to a particular natural place. Little did I know I was already beginning to explore what changing my level of consciousness felt like, induced purely by the natural world and

---

1. Budbill, *Northern Woodlands*, 80.

state of mind, setting the stage for being able to fully engage in future lucid experiences.

To me, sense of place is a deep, heartfelt connection to a particular landscape and the people who inhabit that landscape. It is about the feelings that land creates for me. It is rekindled each time I reconnect with that space and those people. It does not necessarily mean a place is home, but it can feel like home. Sense of place is not always a solitary endeavor for me. When like-minded individuals with a common connection to landscape gather, a collective emotional shift can occur. A kindred group can feel the power of their surroundings and experience deep presence. Sense of place is the intersection of nature, culture, and consciousness shift to being fully present in that place. Sense of place is the comfort I feel when I walk or ski in the forests and fields of my farm.

In the spring and summer of 2009, I walked on the abandoned yet beautiful farm property many times. I came at different times of day to see if there were much road traffic and other annoying sources of noise, such as excessive lawn mowing from adjacent neighbors. There were none. I sat on different hillsides on the property for a variety of views and perspectives of the land. I timed how often a car passed down the road. It averaged about one car an hour. I decided I could live with that. I even camped out on a warm spring evening with my then girlfriend and her friends on the pasture adjacent to the swamp, so we could revel in the glory of the spring peepers' and wood frogs' all-night serenade, as woodcocks and snipes took turns calling from their wet ground nests before launching overhead in the evening for their courtship sky dances. I brought my good friend Kim over to get her thoughts on my prospective new home. We sat on the pasture hill behind the dilapidated farmhouse. She pronounced it tranquil and lay down and took a nap. I knew it was home after it passed my rigorous, albeit eccentric, vetting process. This farm won out over another piece of land just down the road with similar acreage and price tag. That place just didn't have the feeling of home. I felt no connection to that land, no intangible comfort of place.

The old Colgrove Farm was beautiful and inviting, but the farm infrastructure, including the farmhouse, was in disrepair or nonexistent. Frank was not known for his carpentry skills. During the gutting phase of the house project, a good friend, Chuck, offered to let me stay at his place nearby. I had rented out The Holler and new tenants were moving in. I stayed in Chuck's old farmhouse for a few months until the Colgrove house was somewhat livable.

The winter cold stubbornly lingered in late April, like a tenant refusing to leave after being served an eviction notice. Northern Vermont was clobbered by a major snowstorm in the last week of April. Snow clung heavily to the ground, nearly reaching the top of the picnic table in the backyard when I decided to move into my new home. My girlfriend at the time was living in Burlington, and since our relationship was on-again, off-again, I would be moving into my new place alone. I brought some of my clothes contained in heavy-duty garbage bags from Chuck's place to Bear Swamp. I was eager to move in as soon as possible, even if the house wasn't finished. The upstairs had not yet been renovated. The contractors had closed it off with plywood to minimize heat loss, since it had never been properly insulated. And although the basement was mostly finished, it was not yet insulated either and the thirty-year-old furnace struggled to keep the house warm before the woodstove was installed. The kitchen and living room were sealed off with large sheets of plastic in an attempt to contain the sheetrock dust. I would be sleeping in the downstairs bedroom, the one room in the house that was more or less finished, with biting drafts seeping in from both the upstairs and basement on windy days.

When it came time to go to bed on my first night, I was lying there alone, just starting to wander off to sleep as the crescent moon's illumination peeked into the upper pane of the new double-hung bedroom window and onto the freshly finished wide pine floors. The polyurethane smell lingered in the night air. Suddenly, I felt and then saw a wispy white cloud, floating above my head, just over the bed. The cloud then began to form into a rectangular shape, almost that of a refrigerator or washing machine. The shape transformed again, gradually taking on a more human head shape. Eventually, the head clarified into an old woman, with intense, bulging eyes. I realized it was an apparition. I felt its threatening energy and its eyes radiating through me, as if saying to me, "What the hell are you doing in my house?" The ghost form hovered over me and then beside me, next to the bed. My heart raced. I wondered what I had gotten myself into, purchasing this old farmhouse and its scary caretaker. I said to myself, "I am not going to be frightened by this spirit." I needed to show her who was the new boss of this house. I swung my legs out of bed and sat up straight. I attempted to touch the spirit, now directly in front of me. My hands went right through the strange phantom, but she remained still. I told her I was not afraid of her, that this was my house now, and she had to leave if she couldn't stay in peace. I welcomed her to stay if she would be peaceful. The ghost swirled off along the ceiling and disappeared. She has never returned.

As I was overseeing the construction of the farmhouse, the unseasonably cold and snowy April transitioned to a more welcoming mid-May. The amphibians began to return, on what I later learned was a regular schedule. It was rare to see them, but their calls resonated in our natural amphitheater, filling the evening air. First, there were the raspy quacking sounds of the wood frogs, followed shortly thereafter by the high-pitched chorus of spring peepers and then the trills of the tree frogs as spring progressed. During the day, the deep booming, gulping sound marked the arrival of our regular spring and summer resident bird, the American bittern. At about the same time as the bittern's arrival comes the unique sounding bobolink, which nests in the pastures adjacent to our farmhouse. I describe their mid-flight sound to friends as like an analog reel-to-reel recorder being rewound or fast-forwarded, an audio ecstasy. I have come to eagerly anticipate the coming of nature's chorus as it serenades me while I undertake the demanding to-do list of homesteading in spring, and always keep my bedroom window open, allowing the nocturnal spring sounds to lull me to sleep.

I was simultaneously renovating the home and starting the farm back up, while I turned my attention to the needs of the land. My buddy Brandon came to visit Bear Swamp that spring. Brandon had been a soil scientist with the USDA and lived in the Catskill Mountains in New York, about a six-hour drive away. He did not believe me at first when I told him I had beautiful, well-drained, productive soil on the property. He did not think it was geologically possible. He had to see it for himself. Shortly after he arrived, we started auguring some soil test holes. He was shocked. Not one stone, but beautiful well-drained loam. I called a dairy farmer neighbor down the road to till up our first vegetable field. He came over with a three-bottom plow and discs to flip and smooth out the sod. It was a great feeling, that turning over of the soil after years of lying fallow, preparing it for the planting of my first crops.

In one year's time, I was a general contractor, landlord, full-time state employee, boyfriend in a long-distance relationship, and now I was going to try my hand at farming too. Was I entirely crazy?

When I was looking at several different farm possibilities, I asked my friend Chuck, "How do you know when you've found your true home?" He responded, "You just know." I had always lived by the rule "Make the little decisions with your brain and the big decisions with your heart." That is exactly what I did. At that time, I had been living in Vermont for nearly twenty years, bouncing around from place to place across the state, never long enough to settle in. Bear Swamp not only felt like home, but it would be home for the foreseeable future.

I finally found my sense of place, putting down roots for growing old in Judevine.

Bear Swamp Farm (photo credit Jamie Lynn Ryan)

Judevine

© Jim Ryan and Lizzy Mandell

Western sun softly fades
Peepers sing their serenade
Flock of geese flying overhead
Loons are nesting in their beds

Chorus 1
Hoping I might find a sign
That will lead me there to Judevine

I've been outside fighting this cold
This is spring, so I'm told
I am chilled down to the bone
I need the warmth of a hearth and home

Chorus 2
Tell me how long until I find?
Find my way to Judevine

The moon hangs low in a starry night
Led me here to a brand new life
Bear Swamp soothes my wandering soul
Put down roots for growing old

Chorus 3
Down the hollow and open sky
I found my home in Judevine

Scan the QR code to listen to the song,
performed by Lizzy Mandell

My New Old Friend

Bear Swamp Farm, Vermont

Eva smiled broadly when I entered the room. She shared the space with her new roommate Doris, who became her best friend. I found them in their common space sitting next to each other in adjoining chairs, holding hands. She requested that the nursing home attendants bring me dinner as she was served her meal. There was no use in declining her generous offer. Eva could no longer cook; she could at least visit with me over food. Eva preferred to sit on the seat on top of her walker when I visited. She joked that she still had her cat Buster with her. Buster initially came with her to the nursing home. Eva proceeded to lift her walker seat to show me her cat's ashes contained in a pet urn nestled beneath.

Frank and Eva stopped milking cows in the late '80s but raised beef cows and maintained a giant vegetable garden out back for many more years. Eva was known by all the neighbors for her home cooking, baking, and canning all sorts of vegetables and meats. There was never a short visit when guests stopped by at Eva's, especially after Frank died about a decade prior at the age of ninety-three. Eva insisted her visitors stay for lunch or at least for a piece of her legendary homemade apple pie, with apples from the trees out back and the crust made from lard rendered from their own pigs. She often convinced her guests to take on some sort of minor home repair project. Visitors were more than willing to help Eva out so she could continue to stay in the house. When cleaning out and renovating the house, I found dozens of old glass mason jars full of unidentifiable meat and vegetables in the basement pantry. Eva's daughters insisted the house would not be "broom-swept clean," as most purchase and sale agreements require. They let me know, in no uncertain terms, that if I added such a requirement, they would not be selling me the house. They offered to pay for the dumpster but didn't want anything to do with cleaning out their parents' junk.

When cleaning out and renovating the house, I unearthed a half dozen musty photo albums buried in an old kitchen cabinet underneath dusty boxes and ancient, poorly maintained farm equipment in the garage. Within the sticky pages of the weathered albums were photos of Frank tilling soils with a one-bottom plow hitched to their draft horse and maple sugaring with buckets hung on trees, photos of bountiful garden harvests, and images of boisterous card playing at the kitchen table with neighbors. Once a week I took a break as general contractor, overseeing the complete gutting and renovation of the farmhouse, and took one photo album with me to the nursing home. Eva pointed out the characters in each photo, as best as she could remember. She was mentally astute for the most part, with occasional lapses in memory, especially when viewing newer photographs. Her recall was better in remembering her childhood and early days at the farm. I peppered her with questions about how she farmed, her enormous vegetable garden, canning, how many cows she milked, and how they ran their maple sugaring operation, hauling buckets to the wagon and then drawn to the evaporator by horse. We would often laugh at her farm stories, Frank's sense of humor, and her love of farm living. She had lived on the farm for most of her life. I would share my house construction stories with her, and she perked up in excitement thinking about all the renovations to her former home, many of the improvements that she and Frank dreamed about but couldn't afford. After I purchased my first greenhouse, I brought her our tomatoes and salt. The nursing home limited her salt intake; I was smuggling in contraband.

Katie moved in with me about a year after I purchased Eva's place. Katie and I met on a late winter day at a North Country Farming Network meeting being held at a local brewery in Morrisville. The Farming Network was a Heifer International-sponsored organization whose goal was to nurture and facilitate new and small farms in north-central Vermont. When I moved to Lamoille County, I decided to join the local chapter there. I had been homesteading on my previously owned land, The Holler, and had been very active in the budding local food movement in Vermont. Katie had worked for Heifer International some years before and had lived on a farm in Florida and was then running the community garden in Morrisville. After the farmer meeting at the local brewery, Amy, a mutual friend of Katie's and mine, decided to play matchmaker and she gave us each other's contact information. I invited Katie for a homecooked meal at my farm in Wolcott. Part of me knew she wouldn't be able to resist my beautiful new farm homestead, even if she could resist me. It worked, and the rest is history.

I brought Katie with me to visit Eva on several occasions. Katie and I were big hits with Eva and her elderly neighbors. Soon, Eva would insist I give her a big kiss on the lips when I was leaving. She told me she loved me. This was not what stoic New England small dairy farmers were known for.

One day I made calls to the nursing home and Eva's daughter in Florida and asked if it was okay to take Eva on a little field trip. They both replied with enthusiastic yeses and thought it would be uplifting for Eva. It was a year and a half after I purchased the farm, and the first phase of renovations was complete. I wanted Eva to see the house and the farm again. I picked Eva up at the nursing home and drove her to the farm.

When we arrived, I helped Eva up the three stairs on the front porch. She was in awe of all the work we had done. Eva's tiny galley kitchen was now more than double in size, both laterally and vertically. A vaulted pine ceiling hung above, with new granite kitchen counters and hickory cabinets, a store display unit I had purchased for half price. Part of my role as general contractor was construction material clearance sale scavenger. While touring around the first floor of the house, she gazed at the maple flooring unearthed from under the ugly linoleum, and the new wide pine, maple, and ash flooring in the kitchen and bedroom, with a sense of pleasant surprise. I had cut, milled, planed, and joined most of those boards with friends from my forest in Washington, Vermont, and transported them to my new home. For some reason, when Eva and Frank were living in the home, a previous "renovation" included replacing the original farmhouse windows with fewer and smaller windows. I had installed larger windows facing south, which illuminated the entire house. Her eyes popped wide open with admiration of "her" completely refurbished home.

I assisted her back into the vehicle, but this time we headed off in my Ford F-150 four-wheel-drive farm pickup truck. We were off for a cruise around her old farmstead. I took her to the top of the hill behind the house to get the panoramic view of the farm and the bucolic valley it sits in, the same view where I fell in love with the farm on one of my first walks on the land. The place had me in an instant and Eva seemed to share my sentiment, as we sat in the pickup looking out. Eva looked down at the back garden, tilled and full of vegetables, just as she had always done. She looked across the road to see the new greenhouse I had constructed there, now home to tomatoes in summer and winter greens in the colder months. I was putting up cedar post fencing, preparing for the arrival of beef cows, another nod to Eva that I planned on continuing farming the land. Eva said "wow" several times as she beamed at the thought that the recently abandoned farm was again being cared for and would continue on with its new owners.

Eva was thrilled to be back "home" and see all the work we were doing. She seemed reluctant to return to the nursing home when we came back into the house. She lingered in the kitchen. Eva inhaled all the newness and then, as we slowly headed out the front door onto the porch, her eyes swept around the farm, mountains, and pastural fields, as if taking it in for one last time, which, unfortunately, it was. The smile slowly left her face when she knew I would have to bring her back, as nighttime began to fall, casting its shadow on Judevine Mountain. Part of me wanted to adopt Eva on the spot so that she could return to her home. I helped Eva get into my car and as we pulled down the driveway, she looked over her shoulder with a sense of pride at the farm she and Frank lived in and loved for so many decades, now left in my hands to continue. She gently touched my arm and said, "Thank you," as we took the gravel road back to the nursing home.

Eva Colgrove

Katie and I still live on the old Colgrove Farm, which we renamed Bear Swamp Farm. We cut, split, and stack our own firewood from the same woodlot that Frank worked across the swamp. We grow vegetables in our unheated greenhouses, as well as in the same garden out back where Eva tended her vegetables. We have a hundred blueberry bushes, and a dozen beef cows graze our pastures. We sell some of these foods for the local food co-op and to our neighbors, but mostly, it's for ourselves. I planted raspberry bushes and pear, plum, and nut trees when I first moved in, which are now bearing fruit. We still harvest currants from Eva's bushes that Katie makes into jam. Katie cans pickles, dilly beans, fruit jams, tomato sauce, and salsa, just as Eva did.

Eva died at age ninety-five. I am so grateful I had those couple of years to become good friends with her. When I found out about the funeral arrangements, I knew I had to do something at my home—our home—for her. I reached out to her daughters, and suggested Eva's family and friends come to the house after the wake. We would be having homemade apple pie, Eva's favorite, with family and friends.

My New Old Friend

© Jim Ryan and Lizzy Mandell

You tilled the earth and planted the fields
You cooked your friends home-cooked meals
You scythed the grass and harvested hay
Served up your switchel on a hot summer's day

Chorus
You're getting older and your body's worn
You gave up the house where you were born
It's in good hands now, this message I send
Calmy rest, my new old friend
Calmy rest, my new old friend

You hung the buckets and tapped all the trees
You teamed the horses and made all the leads
You cut the wood the old-fashion way
Boiled the sap on a warm spring day

Repeat chorus

Life was hard but you had time for fun
Sing and dance with the setting sun
Up at dawn, you put food away
Warmed by the stove on a cold autumn day

Alternative chorus

Now I'm up before sunrise
Cup of coffee, out the door
I work this land, as you did before
It's in good hands now, this message I send
Calmly rest, my new old friend
Calmy rest, my new old friend

Scan the QR code to listen to the song,
performed by Lizzy Mandell

TRANSFORMATION

The Irish Wake
St. Albans Bay, Vermont

November 2018

I sat in my car for several long minutes before deciding to go in. I was uncharacteristically nervous to see Joanie and the boys, and all my old friends. I was in my head, having second thoughts. I parked my car in one of the spaces reserved for the town-owned dock, which sits directly across the road from the Bayside Pavilion in St. Albans Bay, twenty miles south of the Quebec border. It was late November, in between the two busy seasons of summer boating and winter ice fishing. The full Frost Moon illuminated the skies. I swallowed hard, got out of the safety of my car, as my exhaled breath formed a misty cloud. I crossed the road, and walked into the pub. The Clancy Brothers serenaded the attendees from the pub's sound system. The men in dark suits and ties and the women in black dresses or dress pants warmly conversed. As they settled into the warm, welcoming pub, men loosened their ties and women changed into more comfortable shoes, transitioning from the somber funeral service to a festive celebration of life.

The tiny village of St. Albans Bay consists of a gas station, with attached post office, the Bayside Pavilion, a marina, a town beach and park, and a cluster of historic homes, including our former apartment in a converted old brick farmhouse complex. Max was the postmaster in a one-person post office. It is there where we first befriended Max, when he warmly welcomed us as newbies in town. My then partner Lydia and I both felt his positive aura and energy and witnessed his willingness to help anyone in need. Max was a regular patron at the Bayside. He would go there just about every day after he retired from the Postal Service for lunch and just one or two cocktails. He would always sit in the same seat at the bar. That was Max's seat. Max McKenzie was the person who would be honored at the Bayside Pavilion on this day.

***

When I received the call from Lydia on a chilly evening a few weeks prior, I sat for several seconds in silence as she spoke. She didn't know the cause of Max's death. His friends from the Bayside Pavilion had become concerned when he did not show up. They arrived at his house and found him slumped in his favorite chair, unresponsive. Later, we learned it was likely he had had a heart attack.

Max always seemed to have a twinkle in his eye and a smile on his face, albeit with a subtle devilish grin. Max made anyone he spoke to feel like they were the most important person in the room. Max was a true gentleman in the traditional sense. He would open car doors for elderly women and help them carry their postal packages out to their cars. But Max kept the most coveted space in his heart for Joanie, his second wife.

Joanie was a decade and a half younger than Max. She was

fit and wore small wire-rimmed glasses with her bangs hanging down over them, partially obscuring her face. To those who didn't know her well, she appeared serious, but I knew better. It was true that Joanie counterbalanced Max's dreamer-like qualities with doses of reality. But Joanie wore a set of warm and welcoming dimples that were revealed when she smiled, and she loved to laugh at Max's storytelling. The two glowed in each other's presence and hinted at their teenage libidos, despite their middle-aged-plus years.

During our many social events together, Max loved to recall his college football days, when he attended Columbia University in New York City. Max also played high school varsity basketball and baseball, but football was his passion. He and his brother Pat both played on the Columbia team. He played linebacker for four years and was named to the All-Ivy League team in his junior and senior years. He wore his Irish heritage and pride, both literally and figuratively. His baseball cap of choice was the Fighting Irish, when he wasn't wearing his New York Giants hat. And yes, Max loved his drink. His favorite beverages were Budweiser, Irish whiskey, and Bloody Marys, the latter especially on Sundays.

Sundays were very special for Lydia and me, as we often ventured over to Max and Joanie's place on the eastern shore of Lake Champlain. Their house was a converted summer camp, right across the road from the lake, with their own small beach and a broad view of the water. Max took his time upgrading the camp to a year-round home, doing so over many years. I helped him when I could and offered to be his assistant in getting it done, but Max preferred our company to be purely recreational when we got together.

Joanie and Lydia worked together at the popular seafood restaurant in town. Joanie was the manager there and Lydia waited tables and bartended. Saturday nights, at the end of her restaurant shift, Joanie ordered a very large platter of shrimp cocktail, stuffed grape leaves, local cheeses, spinach and artichoke dip, and antipasto with a loaf of crusty French bread in preparation for our regular Sunday gatherings. Max prepared a batch of his special Bloody Mary homemade mix, as a mad scientist might work with test tubes. It had just enough kick of horseradish, hot sauce, fresh lemon, and Worcestershire sauce. The drink was topped off with several large, pimento-stuffed green olives with a stalk of celery, and, of course, three or four fingers of vodka. I was in heaven and never grew tired of our regular Sunday afternoon meals and beverages.

During the summer months, we would often spend sunny days on their little beach with the perfect sunset view, drinking cold beer and wine. Max and I fished a bit, rarely catching anything, except for an occasional perch when fishing with Max's kids. Max prepared us a delicious fried perch dinner on those days we caught some fish. In the winter months, Max and Joanie loved to watch the New York Giants play football. The Clancy Brothers, Max's favorite Irish band, was always playing at full volume when we arrived at the camp as Joanie and Max were preparing the food and drinks for our visit. Max sang along loudly and passionately.

Evenings and weekends in St. Albans, I rode my bike everywhere. The bike-friendly, gently rolling hills and little car traffic beside the lake lent itself to long rides. I often rode my bike the seven miles to Max and Joanie's place. When I had consumed too many Bloody Marys, I had to stuff my bike in the back of Lydia's car, unable to bike home. I vacationed from my strict diet at the time on the weekends to accommodate our weekend frolics. For the four years that we lived in St. Albans Bay, Max, Joanie, Lydia, and I got together almost every weekend.

Lydia and I first moved to Vermont from Long Island in the fall of 1990. We both fell in love with Vermont, Lydia after attending Lyndon State College in the early 1980s and me after staying at a friend's second home in southern Vermont in the late 1980s. We moved to St. Albans Bay in 1996 for my new job with the US Department of Agriculture as a soil conservationist. It was my first "real" non-restaurant job after I graduated from Johnson State College. Lydia reluctantly moved to St. Albans Bay with me, tolerating several moves across Vermont. We had moved five times in the decade of the 1990s so that I could establish my career in natural resources management. Lydia would have to reestablish herself in yet another location, look for yet another restaurant job, and make new friends. She had reached her moving threshold.

All the moving and focus on my career took a toll on our relationship, and after thirteen years together, Lydia and I broke up in late 1999. I had put our relationship on the back burner and Lydia grew more distant. I was on the education and career path, and she wasn't. She felt she was going nowhere, and she might be slowing me down, even though I didn't feel that way and told her as much. We had a rough and sudden breakup just weeks before we were to move into the first house I purchased. At the last minute, Lydia said she would not be moving with me. She wanted me to cut bait so I could move on with my career without her. All our joint possessions accumulated over thirteen years of living together would have to be sorted and separated at the last minute. I told Lydia to take anything she wanted. I was ready to purge everything. Lydia's stuff headed to storage and mine to the U-Haul truck headed to central Vermont, all on the same day. I was a zombie that day, not fully present and questioning how events and our relationship could unfold so badly. My first home purchase excitement was kiboshed and my psyche crushed.

In the immediate aftermath of the breakup, I moved into my new house and ninety acres of land in Washington, Vermont, about two hours away from St. Albans, alone. Lydia stayed behind, living with a girlfriend, and continued to spend time with Max and Joanie. Because of the rough breakup, I felt awkward about staying in contact with them. I guess this commonly happens with mutual friends when a couple splits up. It is difficult for each of them to stay close friends with past mutual acquaintances. I feared Lydia would not have good things to say about me to Max and Joanie. Because of this unfounded fear, I lost touch with them for nearly twenty years.

Over the years, Lydia and I had become close with Max's three kids from a previous marriage, two sons and a daughter. Just three months before Max's death, his daughter, Molly, died unexpectedly. She had served in the military and struggled with alcohol and drug addiction. Lydia wasn't sure how she died, overdose or suicide, perhaps. She didn't feel comfortable asking, and they hadn't offered an explanation. I deeply regretted not reaching out to Max and Joanie after Molly died.

When Lydia told me about the options for Max's services, which included the wake at the funeral home, the funeral service at the church, and the Irish wake at the Bayside, I chose to attend the latter. I was reluctant to show up at the wake or funeral in those more formal settings after not having seen Joanie in two decades. Irish wakes, a long-held tradition in

Ireland, were typically held in the deceased's home and in some cases, at their favorite pubs, where eating, drinking, and music were featured, all while telling stories of the departed. In Vermont, we have "celebrations of life." Whatever we decided to call this particular gathering, Max would have been pleased.

In the long span of years between our breakup and Max's death, Lydia and I stayed in close contact with each other and enjoyed a deep friendship, despite our ugly ending as a couple. Lydia told me over the phone that she was not feeling well enough to attend any of Max's services. She had been battling ovarian cancer for several years now, undergoing chemo and radiation treatments. After Lydia left Vermont in the early 2000s, she headed back to Long Island to live with her sister and mother in the house she grew up in. She never returned to Vermont. She confessed she had left a part of herself in Vermont, and it would be emotionally unbearable for her to return. I told her I would attend the Irish wake and represent us both.

When I walked into the Bayside for the Irish wake, I saw Joanie at the other end of the bar. Even wearing a black funeral dress, she looked beautiful, with her black hair and those familiar glasses. It looked like she had not aged a bit over the last two decades. She was smiling and talking with a friend. Our eyes met. She broke off the conversation and headed toward me.

Before we uttered any words, we smiled, swung our arms open widely, and deeply embraced. Our arms were wrapped around each other tightly and fully. I had never held anyone the way we hugged on that day. I deeply felt her energy. I absorbed her and she absorbed me. I felt her ribcage. She felt thin. I wept, my body shaking. Joanie began to cry too. I had never openly cried in public before and yet it did not bother me. We sobbed for what seemed like an hour, although it was more likely just a few minutes. Time had screeched to a crawl. It felt like the rest of the pub attendees were blurred out and deep in the background, while Joanie and I, in our embrace, were crystal clear.

It was as if I had not cried in a lifetime, and I was holding back years' worth of tears. Something happened, a switch inside me flipped, and deep and profound emotion was released. I completely surrendered to the sensation and felt at peace with it. Little did I know what was coming in the next several months. This was only the first of several cathartic cries.

I apologized to Joanie for the lack of control of my emotions, especially since Joanie was the one recently widowed. As I finally began to pull myself together, I told Joanie how truly good it was to see her after all these years. There was joy in Joanie's face as she thanked me for being there. My heart lightened. It was as if an emotional anvil had been lifted off my chest.

As Joanie and I uncoupled from our deep embrace and shared our elation in seeing each other again despite the circumstance, Max's two sons, Paddy and Will, approached us. I almost did not recognize them. The last time I saw them, they were teenage boys, and we were fishing together on the lake. Now they were grown men. They called out my name. They saw the tears in my eyes, and I hugged them both. Joanie and the boys walked me over to Max's barstool. The barstool was now adorned with his Fighting Irish cap and his Giants sweatshirt and would later have his name engraved on it. It was Max's stool, after all. Joanie and I exchanged contact information and hugged once more before I slipped out the door.

I headed home from Max's Irish wake, taking the back roads, hugging the Georgia shore of Lake Champlain. I was driving and listening to music. I was trying to process the emotional release that had just unfolded. Just as I was about to take the ramp for the interstate, the song "Fare Thee Well" came on the radio. It was the version performed by Marcus Mumford and Oscar Isaac. I began to shudder and realized I shouldn't be driving in that state. I pulled over and listened to the song in the Maplefields gas-mart parking lot with tears streaming down my face again, twice in one day. The song tells the heartfelt story of leaving a lover behind and the pain felt by that lover, although the "fare thee well" saying might also be thought of as wishing someone well on their journey. I held both thoughts after my Irish wake experience. I reached for my phone from the glove box and emailed Lydia in the parking lot. I recounted the emotional events from the Irish wake, my bittersweet experience seeing Joanie and the boys, and the "Fare Thee Well" song synchronicity. Again, I was psychically crushed by music and interpersonal energies in an emotional epiphany, and Lydia was the person I most wanted to share it with.

Life was so vivid, so clear, so lucid. I was truly living in the moment, feeling every emotion like I had never felt before, surrendering and allowing events to unfold. I wasn't sure if I cried for Max, or for seeing Joanie for the first time in two decades, or for my regret in not communicating with them for so long. After pondering the "why," I began to realize it was an experience of what I can only describe as profound joy. How can all this discussion of sobbing be described as profound joy? For me, it was a deep and meaningful joy to see Joanie, Will, and Paddy after so long, but it was more than that, too. I realized I found joy in surrendering, acceptance, and forgiveness.

With that realization, I forgave myself for being an absent

friend. I freed myself from the guilt of not reaching out to Max and Joanie when their daughter died tragically. I absolved Lydia for hurting me so deeply during our breakup. I unburdened myself for hurting her and for holding on to that feeling for so long. Finally, the energetic logjam was released in a cascade of healing emotion.

Max, Lydia, Jim, and Joanie—Sunday brunch

The Irish Wake

© Jim Ryan

Old friend, I heard you passed away
You didn't show up at the pub that day
They found you in your favorite chair
Your daughter's sudden death you couldn't bear

Your Irish wake at the same pub, on the bay
Just across from where you worked, every day
The Clancy Brothers playing when I arrived
When you sang those songs, you were so alive

Chorus
They all gathered in their dresses and suits
With drinks in their hands and tears in
    their eyes
They shared funny stories and sang all your
    songs
You shined a light on so many lives

Your wife's eyes caught me from across the room
A cold November night on the full moon
We collapsed into each other's arms
I shuddered in her deep embrace and calm

Repeat chorus

I felt so close to you again leaving the bar
On my way home from the wake in my car
The song Fare Thee Well brought me to tears
Where had I been for all those years?

Outro
Old friend, I heard you passed away
Fare Thee Well, is all I can say

Angola, Cuba

Eastern Cuba

December 2018

The airplane taxied on the tarmac and the airport workers rolled the portable staircase up to the plane. When the plane door opened, we were welcomed by a sultry and sweet-smelling breeze and temperatures in the low eighties. Palm and coconut trees ringed the airport, with brightly colored flowering orchids in the quasi-shade of their understory, the source of the sweetness.

Brandon and I and the rest of the passengers on board arriving in Holguin, Cuba, from Montreal, Quebec, stepped down the boarding stairs. We walked across the tarmac toward the airport entrance single file. Once inside, we were serenaded by a live Cuban band playing traditional Cuban "Son" music, the type of music made famous in the *Buena Vista Social Club* film. While we were in line waiting to be processed by the Cuban authorities, smiling women in short skirts and fishnet stockings floated around with trays of rum and Cokes, offering them to the newly arrived. Brandon and I looked at each other, smiling. Our plane was a time machine transporting us back to a more nostalgic 1960s. Just outside the airport doors, drivers of pastel-painted classic 1950s American cars offered taxi rides, and Cubanos walked along the edges of highways, being passed by horseback riders and ox-cart drivers and motorcyclists, most riding two-up and without helmets. The portal door to a parallel universe had been opened, once again, although this one was completely different than the door that opened on our trip to Death Valley (described in the "Saline Skies" essay).

Brandon received the signal for us to return to Cuba for his second and my fourth trip there. The Universe presented him with a not-so-subtle message while he was traveling in Key West. He felt compelled to find a peaceful and meditative activity on the water. He opted for a paddleboard rental in a quiet shallow bay near an accessible float-up bar on a boat. Shortly after he set off with the stand-up paddleboard, and within earshot of the bar, he heard the familiar, welcoming sounds of the soundtrack from the *Buena Vista Social Club* bathe over him. On our first trip to Cuba, I had suggested he listen to this culturally significant soundtrack as part of his introduction to Cuban culture. The mix of the driving percussion and haunting trumpet accompaniment with the grizzled and sultry vocals went right through him. As he was serenaded by the "Son" music, he gazed down in the water and noticed a red starfish lying on the sand below. He was triggered both auditorily and visually. He was reminded of our first trip to Cuba when we rented sea kayaks and paddled on a remote cove and were welcomed by dozens of starfish. He must return to Cuba.

Brandon and I enjoyed traditional Cuban music, not only in how it sounds, but for the effect and impact music has on its people and culture. We saw it firsthand, time and time again. When the music comes on it is like a cue, a prompt to transition. Within moments of music filling the air, the rum and beers shortly follow. Soon thereafter, dancing begins. Cubanos dance with such passion, most evident in the movement of their swaying hips. Smiles and laughter come easily. Cubanos of all ages dance with reckless abandon alone and with each other. It doesn't matter what day of the week or time of day. When the music comes on, everyday lives are put on hold, and they celebrate and transcend.

During this second trip to Cuba together, we would celebrate Brandon's fiftieth and my fifty-fourth birthday, as well as Christmas and New Year's. Brandon and I both knew intuitively that our second visit to Cuba was going to be even more special than a previous one. The year before, on our first joint trip to Cuba, Brandon and I had attended an international agroecology conference with visits to local innovative farms. We are both small farmers and have been involved in the sustainable agriculture movement for many years. As much as we had enjoyed the first trip, it was a bit too structured for us, and we both had come down with bad colds and gastrointestinal illnesses, which dampened our naturally over-the-top enthusiasm levels. For our second trip we needed to do what we do best, free flow and jump from boulder to boulder, or, in other words, to "Zen travel," as we did on our trip to Death Valley. We would be going to eastern Cuba, which was off the beaten path for most tourists. We wanted to experience "real

Cuba" and not be bound by any sort of structured or preplanned trip.

Our two weeks in Cuba felt like two months. It was difficult for both of us to keep track of which day it was. Time went from the objective clock time to the subjective spiritual time. We connected deeply with strangers we encountered along the way, and then would drive just twenty miles down the road to have new experiences with different strangers. The new encounters felt separate and unique from the previous ones, but with an underlying theme of openness to possibilities.

Jim and Brandon on the beach in Cuba (photo credit Jim Ryan)

The aura of our positive energy and enthusiasm was contagious and spread to those around us, to otherwise complete strangers that we encountered along the way. We were completely open to it all and were deeply rewarded in turn. As Brandon and I were walking down the sidewalks in the city of Holguin, he felt a strong pull to go inside a darkened building full of old books, and I obliged. We encountered a gatekeeper of sorts at the entrance to the building, the head librarian at the front desk. Anna worked long hours with little pay "protecting" (her word) the library and its understocked shelves and outdated books.

When we were seeking some limes for our rum drinks, outside of Baracoa, we befriended the street fruit vendor Joel, who was supporting his widowed dad financially. As we walked along a seaside road, we crossed paths with the only jogger we saw on the entire trip. We named him "George Foreman," because of his remarkable resemblance to the former boxing champion. He liked the new name bestowed upon him.

"George Foreman" and Jim (photo credit Brandon Dennis)

After Brandon's fiftieth birthday dinner, and under the influence of wine and beer, we went for a walk in downtown Baracoa beneath the nearly full moon. Brandon scaled up onto an historic garrison museum wall to get a closer look inside. I followed behind Brandon, hoping to convince him to turn around. Little did we realize the garrison museum was protected twenty-four hours a day by two guards, who approached us, stunned that these American tourists would trespass at such an hour. I thought we would be experiencing a real Cuban jail in our near future. I had to think fast. Smiling broadly, I explained that my good friend had too much to drink at his special fiftieth-birthday celebration. I added some fictional details that Brandon was an amateur historian wanting a closer look at this well-preserved historically signifi-cant site. The serious demeanor of the guards soon faded, and the three of us began to joke, initially at Brandon's expense. The Cuban guards then suddenly pivoted the conversation to share how beautiful the Cuban women are, as almost a form of national pride. Soon the four of us were laughing loudly. I was relieved Brandon and I were not getting arrested and spending time in a Cuban jail cell after all.

One of these encounters with our new Cuban friends was foreshadowed in a precognition dream. I was jarred from the dream right around sunrise at one of our casa stays. Brandon was already awake and stirring around our room. In the transi-tional state between deep sleep and wakefulness, I experienced a vivid vision. In this quasi-dream state, I visualized a Cuban woman. My memory was vague in the context of why she was visiting me in my dream, but specific in her physical details: she was young, early twenties, Black, petite, with short hair and a radiant, welcoming smile. I hopped out of bed as I shared this lucid dream with Brandon, including my detailed description of the young Cuban woman, as he listened intently.

After breakfast, we decided to walk over to a small resort located half a mile just west of our casa location. The high-end boutique resort was encircled with a compound fence to keep the locals out for the guests' "safety." We, on the other hand, fully embraced the Cubanos and their culture and hospitality and felt more comfortable in their presence than with the exclusive resort crowd, but we needed to use the resort's Wi-Fi. Brandon and I walked over to the resort to have a drink and check our email. After we dealt with our "real world" tasks and were walking along the dirt road back to our casa, we were approached by two Cubana women selling sweet dessert treats.

I was stopped in my tracks, literally, when I realized the younger of the two was the same woman I had dreamt about only hours beforehand. I engaged the women in conversation in Spanish and translated for Brandon. After I realized that neither spoke any English at all, I said to Brandon, "Oh my God, it is the identical woman from my vivid dream just a few hours ago." I made direct eye contact with the younger woman and subtly smiled, as if to acknowledge the secret of our "shared" previous experience, already meeting in my dream.

I purchased some of the treats they were selling, hoping to learn more about the woman from my dreams. Her name was Ta Ta. She was a single mom, shedding her abusive boyfriend and father of her ailing son, who required daily medication for an undisclosed illness. She had recently lost her home in a hurricane and was living nearby in temporary housing provided by the government. She was working several jobs, making and selling baked goods, cooking in a local restaurant, and being a massage therapist for tourists staying at the resort. Her multiple jobs provided additional income so she could rebuild her destroyed home, literally one brick at a time. My ears perked up when I heard the word "massage," as my body was aching. I proposed to Brandon that we sign up for some birthday massages on the beach with Ta Ta. She obliged and we made back-to-back appointments for the following day. It was as if I were living in both my everyday and a higher level of consciousness at the same time. Brandon and Ta Ta were my copilots on this otherworldly ride into the numinous, as we were becoming friends with a character from my lucid dream.

Ta Ta and Brandon (photo credit Jim Ryan)

In each of these interactions with complete strangers, Brandon and I were able to transcend their initial stoicism and guarded personalities. Anna, Joel, George Foreman, Ta Ta, and even the museum guards opened their hearts to us, invited us to their homes, asked us to attend a classical music concert and to go out to the local nightclubs. We were guests at a Christmas Eve church service in a ramshackle building attached to a sawmill in the middle of a forest. The holiday service was full of passionate singing, a live gospel band, a bit of dramatic theater, and spiritual healing ceremonies. We spent Christmas evening on the beach, enjoying a dried palm frond bonfire, celebrating with our Cuban host family. One of the museum guards even showed us a picture of his eighteen-year-old niece he wanted to set us up with. We politely declined his generous offer.

Our Cuban friends had little from a material or financial perspective, but what they had, they gladly shared with us. Neither did they expect anything from us. They simply craved our friendship. On our last day with each of our new friends, we left them with Cuban money. We had intentionally waited until the last time we saw them, so our experiences would not be tainted with the prospect of payment. The money became a parting and unexpected gift. We helped Anna, the librarian, take a well-deserved respite from the library to visit a sick aunt near Havana. We gifted money to Ta Ta, the massage therapist, to buy a small refrigerator to keep her son's medicine cold and to purchase some bricks for her new home. We took Joel, the fruit vendor, and George Foreman, the jogger, out for nights on the town. We generously tipped all our casa host families.

As rewarding as these experiences and interactions were, they left us both emotionally exhausted. We had thought that when we moved to a different area or town or new casa, we would be given a brief emotional reprieve, if only to catch our breath. That did not turn out to be the case.

Anna, the librarian, and Jim (photo credit Brandon Dennis)

Our Zen trip moved to the next phase, when we hoisted our backpacks and rode our moped to the village of Maguana, twenty miles or so northwest of Baracoa, and our next destination, Carlos's seaside casa. Maguana is located next to the 274-square-mile Alejandro de Humboldt National Park. It is a UNESCO World Heritage Site known for its unique flora, fauna, and biodiversity. It provided us with a tropical and peaceful setting. Our accommodation was an airy, white-painted bungalow with high ceilings and a thatched roof with two beds, a small fridge, and a bathroom. It was located about fifty feet from Carlos's family's house. In the space between Carlos's house and our bungalow casa were a family of pigs and a flock of chickens, all roaming freely.

Brandon and I quickly settled into our new space and then

headed to a little palm-thatch-covered cabana where our meals were served, overlooking a beautiful seaside cove with five hundred feet of golden sand and warm turquoise waters. There was only one other home, besides Carlos's, in the cove that was encircled with palm and coconut trees. We ordered a round of strong rum, coconut, and honey drinks from Carlos's wife, Maria. The beautiful setting almost insisted we stay longer. We checked to see if we could stay two days more in Zen-like fashion. After we secured the additional nights' stay, we put on our bathing suits and went for a swim, riding the waves until dinner. We returned to the sea for more body surfing after a delicious lobster dinner, caught in the same cove we were now swimming in. We swam under the watchful eye of the full moon as I declared, "This is my best birthday ever!" We both acknowledged our perception of time had dramatically slowed, and so we began to rest emotionally. Or so we thought.

Brandon and I had such a relaxing and fun time on our first day at our cabana paradise that we thought we would just duplicate it the next day. After lunch we decided to start happy hour early. We set up Brandon's portable speaker and iPod, grabbed cold beers from our bungalow's college-dorm-sized fridge, and headed for the cabana perched over the beach. We began our launch (as we like to call the start of happy hour) as we normally do, diving deep into the music. We were beginning to feel the buzz that would take us to our happy place. We had all the important ingredients in place—stunning tropical beach setting, temperatures in the eighties, music, beer, and our mutually energetic connection. We were doing what we did best. In the next few minutes, our world was about to be rocked.

From the corner of my eye, I noticed someone walking down the beach. He was several hundred feet away, moving toward us very slowly. He was carrying a bag over one shoulder and was walking with a significant limp, heavily favoring one side. I warned Brandon someone was headed our way, ready to sell us his wares. We had experienced some unpleasant sales harassment in our previous stay in Baracoa, so we kept our focus on the music and beers, hoping the person would just continue down the beach past us. Instead, when he drew even with the cabana, he began heading up the half dozen steps from the beach that lead up to us. He struggled up the stairs as Brandon and I watched, as he made his way, pulling the bad leg up the stairs with the assistance of his hands, one step at a time. He seemed determined. Our music remained on while we witnessed the scene unfolding in front of us. We glanced at each other, as if saying, "What is going on here? All this work, just for a quick sale?"

The man must have been in his late sixties or early seventies, although it was hard to tell given his condition. He started speaking to us in Spanish and I did my best to interpret what he was saying. My Spanish skills are mediocre at best, and his slurred speech made it even more challenging. I began to wonder if he'd had a stroke, between his challenging communication and trouble using one side of his body. He struggled to take his canvas bag off his shoulder as we stood by silently and watched every move he was making.

He finally hefted the bag to the ground and inside it were several ripped plastic bags holding random items. Brandon and I thought these were the wares he wanted to sell. But we were wrong. First, he showed us a photo. It appeared to be 1980s vintage. The photo was of a dark-skinned Cuban man surrounded by African men, women, and children, all happily smiling, with arms around each other. Then he pulled out another plastic bag. He was struggling to open it, so I helped him. Inside his torn bag was a medal. Then he pulled out another bag, revealing a letter with a photo of Fidel Castro. It was an award letter that must have come with the medal. After some back-and-forth conversation, I pieced together that he had served with the Cuban army in the Angola Civil War to support that government in its fight with South African troops aligned with the US. He had been wounded and was honored for his service by the Cuban government. The young Cuban man in the photo in Africa was him. He was sharing with us his pride for having served his country with honor.

Brandon and I finally turned off the music to be fully present and listen to his story. We offered him a beer and he declined. Instead, he offered us one of his few cigarettes. We politely declined his cigarettes but pulled out our own, which we only smoke on these special occasions, so that we could smoke with him. I asked if he was married and where he lived and translated his answers for Brandon. He told us he lived in a nearby village with his wife and he walked around the village and up and down the beach every day.

I looked down and noticed he was wearing cheap mismatched flip-flops, both in rough shape and one with a very large hole in it. And then I glanced down at my brand-new Keen sandals lying on the ground next to him. I had just purchased them prior to our trip. I knew at once what had to be done. I first asked the man if he would like a new pair of shoes and then pointed to my sandals. He nodded yes. One of his feet was extremely swollen. Because our new friend had trouble balancing, he struggled with the task of taking off his sandals and putting on his new ones. Brandon and I, both without words, moved in to help him. We had to adjust the Keen sandals' straps to accommodate his swollen foot and help slide his feet into them. They fit perfectly. He seemed grateful, although it was hard to gauge his reaction.

It was then I noticed my eyes had begun to fill with tears. I forgot I was in the company of Brandon. I swiped at the tears, trying to hide them from him. When I looked up, I saw that Brandon, too, had tears streaming down his face. We had been friends for nearly twenty-five years, and we had never cried in front of each other until then.

Something shifted in us personally, in our friendship, in that experience of deep presence. It was an otherworldly feeling, like being visited by a ghost. This stranger had appeared, offered us a look at his most intimate possessions from a small sack, and had left just as elusively, shuffling off up the hill. We both watched him limp off in silence while the tears continued to flow from our eyes. We looked at each other, as if to say, "Did that really just happen?"

We felt a deep bond with and compassion for this complete stranger as he shared his life story with us and wanted nothing from us in return, except our time. It was a surreal twenty-minute eternity, almost an out-of-body sensation. It was almost as if we were watching this scene from above. We were participants in an event where someone else, or more likely, some*thing* else, was controlling how the event unfolded. It felt like an intervention. Brandon and I were shaken to the core. We completely surrendered to the feeling, our senses heightened and followed our instincts. Giving the stranger my brand-new sandals seemed like such a small gesture, but it felt like we brought him happiness, at least temporarily. What it brought us was much greater.

We saw Carlos, our casa host, watching this scene in real time from outside his house smoking a cigarette. He had previously protected us from many of the locals wanting to sell their wares to his guests. He would normally shoo them away, but he had allowed the Angolan War veteran to approach us. Carlos came over to us and smiled. We were intrigued to learn more of the stranger's story and asked Carlos to fill in the blanks. Carlos confirmed the stranger had served valiantly in the Angolan Civil War and had been severely wounded. It was likely he suffered from post-traumatic stress disorder. Carlos also shared that the veteran struggled with alcohol abuse and several health issues upon his return home to Cuba from Angola. He had stopped drinking, but he recently had a stroke. Nonetheless, he continued to walk most days around town and on the beach. Carlos thanked us for our kindness to the stranger.

"Angola" with his new sandals (photo credit Brandon Dennis)

I hadn't been able to understand the stranger's name when he shared it with us. His name would forever be Angola to Brandon and me. We were deeply humbled; we had misjudged the veteran. We decided we would never do that again.

After our epic adventure and deep connections with our new Cubano friends, we decided we needed to do more, to give back, to serve those in need. I would personally make volunteer service my priority, after I left my current job. I would pay it forward, since we were the ones who received the gifts, the lessons of humility and compassion.

Angola

© Jim Ryan

We were minding ourselves, drinking our booze
On vacation, listening to tunes
Our lives about to be changed forever
By a man with holes in his shoes

We watched you hobble down the white sand
Your life's possessions in your mangled hand
Your body was broken, but you had such
*   strong will*
Pictures of you in African lands

Chorus
Angola, we are haunted by the ghost of you
Now we know what we're supposed to do

You slurred your words and struggled with
*   speech*
But you struck a chord within us so deep
Now our lives would never be the same
You shared the pain and secrets that you keep

Repeat chorus

For a few moments, time stood still
Our first-world problems were just silly fears
You left us humbled and full of respect
Two grown men broke down in tears

Bridge
Pay it forward, the gift of our time
With open hearts and open minds

Alternative chorus
Angola, we are haunted by the ghost of you
Now we know what we're supposed to do

You Made a Difference
Elmore and Wolcott, Vermont

February 2019

The streetlight's illumination outside the front window reflected off the glistening road surface. The roads were becoming a sheet of black ice, the most treacherous driving conditions in the North Country, where you have little or no control of your vehicle, no matter what you are driving. I was going to be stuck at my friend Sean's house until conditions improved, which did not seem likely to happen any time soon. I paced back and forth, going from room to room, looking out different windows, as sportscasters bantered about statistics and which players to watch out for. It was Super Bowl Sunday. Sean invited me over to watch the game with a couple of friends. I typically don't watch football; in fact, I don't even own a TV, but I agreed to go for the social aspect of it. Imagine the juxtaposed scene, friends enthusiastically watching the big game, while I was lost in my head, and trapped in my friend's house, wondering and worrying if Lydia was still alive.

Earlier that day, I felt very off, my body tired and run down, I had bouts of nausea. I thought I was coming down with a stomach bug that was going around. The feelings of tiredness and nausea transitioned to chest pains. I was beginning to wonder what the hell was going on. After an initial panic that maybe I was having a heart attack, I realized it was more of a feeling of persistent tenderness in my sternum and into my stomach, which was strange since I hadn't physically injured myself recently.

I decided I would shower and try to rally and head to Sean's Super Bowl party. I needed a distraction and the comfort of friends. On the way to Sean and Nancy's house my cell phone pinged. My cell phone doesn't work at my house, or my friends' house for that matter. But I can usually get two bars of signal for about a half mile before fading out on the way to Sean's place. I pulled over to the side of the road to retrieve the message. I noticed it was a 631 area code—Suffolk County, Long Island. I knew it could not be good news. It was Marie, Lydia's sister. Marie's trembling voice said, "We called an ambulance late this morning to take Lydia to the hospital; she was having trouble breathing." After a long pause, she choked out, "She probably won't make it through the night." It was 6:00 in the evening—hours since that message had been sent— so I wasn't sure if Lydia was still alive. I desperately tried to call Marie back. I left several frantic messages. Marie was not answering the phone or returning my calls. The weather suddenly began to shift from rain to freezing rain. I was only a half mile from Sean and Nancy's place, so I decided to try Marie from their landline.

It took me several hours to realize that the pain and feeling of doom I had been experiencing was the prelude to Lydia's impending death. When the light bulb went off for me that day, it reaffirmed all my fears. Something was deeply wrong; something bad was about to happen. Lydia was trying to send me a message over the two hundred and fifty miles that separated us. Lydia and I shared the gift of intuition and precognition. I shouldn't have been surprised that, in the moment of her death, her consciousness would try to communicate with me. There are many scientists who study what happens to people as they die and believe our consciousness is separate from our brain and body and that we take our consciousness with us after death.[1] You are your consciousness, and consciousness is like energy. Energy cannot be destroyed; it can only change form. The belief that your consciousness is immortal formed the basis for my own spirituality, as it did for Lydia. If I couldn't communicate with Lydia in the traditional sense, I wanted to be able to communicate with her consciousness.

I looked out the window again at Sean and Nancy's place and noticed a thick glaze of ice coating the power lines. My uneasy mood could not bear sitting idly by. I had to do something. I needed to get home, despite the road conditions and Nancy's suggestion that I sleep on the couch. At least driving home was doing something. The town roads resembled an ice-skating rink with a sheening frozen glaze on the travel lane. I drove a few hundred feet, and the car began sliding to the left, and I nearly did a one-eighty. I cursed the town road guys and

---

1. Meadows, *The Medicine Way*.

thought they must have taken the Super Bowl evening off, since there was no evidence of road salt or sand. Dreading a very steep hill a mile ahead, I continued in the direction that the one-hundred-eighty-degree spin had pointed the car and headed the few hundred feet back to the state highway. I thought there would be a better chance the state road crews were on duty, despite this unofficial holiday evening. The detour and poor road conditions made the drive home a nail-biting, nearly one-hour ride from hell.

I collapsed into bed, but I did not sleep much that night; my body was exhausted, but my head was spinning. I was up early to call Marie to confirm what I already knew: Lydia had passed the night before, around 7:00. Through choking tears, I asked Marie what Lydia's last days and hours were like. Marie confided, as I feared, that Lydia died alone in the hospital. I offered to call my family and some of Lydia's Vermont friends to give them the terrible news.

The call to Lydia's best friend in Vermont, Joanie, was particularly difficult. Joanie had just lost her husband, Max, two and a half months prior and her stepdaughter, Molly, a few months before that (described in "The Irish Wake" essay). Lydia had been too sick to attend Max's funeral in Vermont, and I offered to go and represent both of us. Lydia kept in touch with Max and Joanie regularly over the years and remained close—closer than I had, in fact. When I reached Joanie, I blurted out I had some terrible news to share: Lydia had died the night before. We both lost it, sobbing over the phone. My mind flashed back to the deep embrace we shared just two and a half months prior at Max's Irish wake celebration of life. I wanted to share that feeling with her again. I told Joanie I was sending her that same heartfelt squeeze over the phone. We both needed it. I called my family and a handful of our friends, trying as best I could to hold it together, losing my composure nearly every time.

I called in sick to work for an entire week after Lydia's death. My stomach had been tied up in knots. I could not eat much, which is extremely uncharacteristic of me. I knew I would not be able to put on a happy face and pretend all was well. I am someone who is not exactly known for putting his emotions on display for the world to see, but I knew I could break down at any moment. I needed to sequester myself in the safety of my home.

My first impulse upon hearing the news was that I desperately wanted to see Lydia, talk to her, and email her. My rational side knew this was not possible. So, I did the next best thing I could think of. I had several boxes of photos buried in a closet upstairs. I spent a morning unearthing the dusty boxes and pulling out any photo of Lydia I could find. It had been nearly twenty years since we had broken up, and I had not looked at those photos in well over a decade, probably longer.

I painstakingly went through each photo: the one of us vacationing on a Mexican beach, Lydia proudly embracing me at my college graduation, Lydia hugging my mom next to the van with my brother Chris and sister-in-law Teresa, heading to a whitewater tubing adventure in the Catskills, and Lydia getting a shamrock painted on her face one St. Patrick's Day with my father and close friends in Stowe. The unposed photo of Lydia and me captured at Robert Moses beach a few months after we started dating, in a funny, happy embrace of new love, particularly crushed me. It was a perfect representation of the infatuation in early romance.

Lydia and Jim at Jim's college graduation.

I had to have these pictures near me in the weeks following her death. They were displayed on the kitchen table, next to my laptop. I placed a photo of her in my car near the shifter, so I could see her when I was on the road. I also pulled out some of "our" CDs: Steely Dan, Old and in the Way, the Rolling Stones, and The Band. I tuned in to the 1st Wave station on the radio; more of our favorite music. Being surrounded by the music and photos from our time together provided an audiovisual comfort blanket.

Even though we had broken up all those years ago and Lydia moved back to Long Island in the early 2000s, our friendship deepened, and we stayed in touch regularly by phone and email. During more recent years, Lydia would often prompt me about recalling some of our fond memories together, like she was gathering them up to take with her on her journey. She knew she was dying, and she was allowing her memories of our good times together to wash over her through our conversations. I remember wondering, "Why all the nostalgia?" while on one of those calls, since I did not know her cancer was terminal. In one such call Lydia asked, "Do you remember when we went out to that fancy seafood restaurant near the ocean for a lobster dinner? You had a hell of a time cracking open the lobster claw, after we shared a bottle of champagne. I remember the claw launching backwards over your shoulder and us both cracking up uncontrollably. The guy sitting at the next table came over to us with the claw in hand, asking if we lost something!" It was one of the many silly and fun moments in our relationship.

It had been years since I had seen Lydia in person, although I tried many times to connect with her on one of my regular trips to Long Island to visit my family. Lydia was too proud for me to see her in the feeble, swollen condition as she suffered through chemo and radiation treatments for her ovarian cancer. Yet Lydia was my spiritual soulmate, sharing our sense of "knowing" when something bad might be happening to our close family or friends hundreds of miles away or even with each other. We always seemed to know what the other was thinking throughout our relationship and in our close friendship that followed until her death.

On a sunny, warm spring day a few months after Lydia left this world, Marie and Lydia's mom, Rose, requested I say something about Lydia at an informal service for her at the home the three of them shared on Long Island. Several of Lydia's close friends and family would be attending. Shortly before they were going to gather the attendees in the sunroom for me to speak, Marie handed me a note she found in Lydia's bedroom after she died. She said, "You better wait until after you speak before you read it." I recognized the handwriting; it was a note from Lydia to me. I knew I had to read it right then and there. Marie was correct, I should have waited to read it. I had to walk around the block to gather myself before I spoke at the event. Lydia's note read:

"It's funny, years and years may pass.
A lot of things change.
But what is amazing is that there are people who,
are simply planted within your heart and will never fade away
no matter what.
Memories that will stay with you forever.
A person who you thought would always be your soulmate.
Then not. Then yes. Forever.
Although your life and theirs have changed.
There is always a voice inside of your head, and a feeling inside
your heart that says,

I will LOVE you forever.
Yes, I will."

The note reaffirmed my deep spiritual connection with Lydia. I knew we would continue our relationship, even after Lydia entered the spirit world.

While Lydia's death was soul-crushing for me, her dying was like hitting the life "reset button." In the weeks and months following her death, I released emotion, creativity, passion, and enthusiasm for life in an extremely intense way. I wrote song lyrics about my lucid life experiences, collaborating with seasoned musicians to bring those words to life in song. What was deep inside me for years needed to come out.

I have never experienced such profound openness before. I reached out to close family and friends at a much deeper level. I took them along on my mystical magic carpet ride. Those closest to me responded in kind, sharing some deeply held secrets. I wrote and spoke to them from my heart. I cried aloud, both in person and on the phone. I had never done anything like that before. I had been too proud, too stubborn, too emotionally elusive. I called our mutual friend Leona from upstate New York to inform her of Lydia's death. I hadn't spoken to her for nearly twenty-five years. The three of us worked together in the same restaurant on Long Island in the late 1980s. We spent an hour and a half on the phone, sharing memories and tears and have remained connected ever since.

After some research, I later discovered others have described similar awakening experiences like Miller and C'de Baca's[2] quantum change or Maslow's[3] peak experiences, sudden and profound emotional and/or mystical events that can cause major life transformations. My moment was a series of moments unfolding over a three-month period in the late fall and early winter of 2018 and 2019. The events started at an Irish wake to celebrate the passing of my estranged friend Max (described in "The Irish Wake" essay), followed a few weeks later with an epic adventure to eastern Cuba with my buddy Brandon (described in the "Angola, Cuba" essay), and a month after that, the finale, the death of Lydia. To me, these events are forever linked together. These three events were like a defibrillation, bringing me back to being more fully present in my life.

---

2. Miller and C'de Baca, *Quantum Change*.
3. Maslow, *Religions, Values, and Peak Experiences*.

These emotionally jarring experiences, one right after the other over a short period of time, profoundly changed my life course. The events themselves were the clear starting point of transition, but to this day, that transformation is still occurring, albeit at a less jarring pace.

During our rough breakup period, when her self-confidence hit rock bottom, Lydia once told me her life did not make a difference to anyone. I knew that wasn't true and told her as much. I reminded her about her tenderness and care for her dying "Oma," also from ovarian cancer, for over two years; her volunteer work at the local senior center and garden club; and the kindness she showed me in our time together. Lydia's life made a difference, to me, and her death transformed me. Once I let go, so much came out in such a positive way. It came unexpectedly and there was no turning back.

I changed. I changed on the inside.

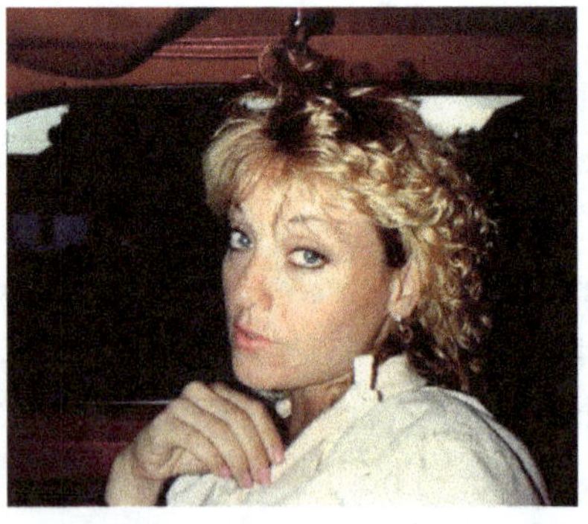

Christine Lydia Liske (photo credit Jim Ryan)

You Made a Difference

© Jim Ryan and Scott Graner

Something felt so deeply wrong
Dark skies suddenly filled my door
Freezing rain soaked into snow
Icy rivers flowed over their banks
Winter clouds lingered so low
Your passing I felt, and now I know

I've never cried so hard before
The tears just stream down my cheeks
Could happen now at any time, any other place
I surround myself with images of you
Kiss those pictures of your face
And anywhere you left your trace

Chorus
You made a difference
You'll never know
Turn this sorrow to strength
Learn from you, we'll all grow
And the sun will shine through my door

Your piercing blue eyes could see right
    through me
If the world could only see
Our current runs so strong, so deep
You were so kind to the old
Now, you'll never grow old
But your story will be told

Repeat chorus

Scan the QR code to listen to the song audio,
performed by Scott Graner

4,000 Weeks

Popham Beach, Maine

January 2023

It was one of the coldest weekends in recent record. We set up our lobster cookout behind the dunes, which provided a wind break of sorts from the brutal, fierce winds. The shelter of the dunes allowed us to use our propane tank to boil our fresh-purchased Maine lobsters and mussels in water collected from the sea. Zach Bryan's *American Heartbreak* album on a portable speaker provided the audio backdrop to our insane seafood celebration.

After fortifying ourselves with ample alcohol lubricants, John, Joe, Leanne, Brandon and I proceeded to walk, some might say march, with determination, the quarter mile out to an island that was only accessible at low tide, for a sunset happy hour. We dubbed this spit of land Ghost Rider Island, after the sacred space the five of us had created on the top of Brandon's Catskill mountaintop. Ghostland has since become a place to set intentions, mourn the dead, play live music, perform theatrical acts, and practice our pagan/Buddhist/Native American mix of nature-based spirituality.

We stood atop a rock outcrop fifteen hundred feet from shore, while both the northern wind and my wild comrades and I howled simultaneously. We huddled together, inadequately dressed, challenging the minus-twenty-degree windchill as darkness descended and rising tides began to surround our island. My ever-rational mind resurfaced from its temporary departure to insanity, imagining an impossible overnight island stay or a bone- chilling swim. I contemplated whether we would freeze to death or drown or suffer the humiliation and cost of a Coast Guard rescue attempt on this bitterly cold January day. I prompted the crew with my sense of urgency, as the sea circled, and nighttime fell. Meanwhile, my friends were shouting with joy, taking turns hoisting a flaming homemade trident, defying the weather gods.

Leanne, Jim, Brandon, John, and Joe on Ghost Rider Island, Popham Beach, Maine (photo credit Leanne Nabinger)

Our island adventure nearly ended badly, as we had to wade through the stiff current and knee-deep incoming frigid tides. We were close to the point of no return in making it back to shore in near-total darkness, emerging from the relentless sea with less than fifteen minutes to spare, wet, cold, and elated.

I had driven to Maine solo from northern Vermont, since the rest of the contingent would be coming from upstate New York. While driving the four and a half hours to Maine, a list of intentions suddenly came to me. Creative inspiration often comes to me during long drives. I had to pull over and write them down in the little notebook I keep in my glove box for such brainstorms. Before leaving for my trip, I read the *New York Times*'s book review[1] of *Four Thousand Weeks—Time Management for Mortals*.[2] I was struck by seeing in print the average human lifespan expressed in weeks and was thinking about that during the drive. I never read the book, nor found the need for guidance on how to manage my time. But that statistic—the brief duration of the average lifespan—stuck with me. It led me to circle back in my mind to how much time I was spending in a job that was causing me great stress. The inspiration of an epiphany struck. At the end of our epic and brutally cold long weekend on the coast of Maine, I shared my epiphany and list with my Catskill Mountain friends.

My list of intentions included wellness, adventure, service, gratitude, creativity, and humility and started and ended with freedom. It was not freedom in a political sense, which we hear

---

1. Williams, "Life is Short. What Are You Going to Do About That?"
2. Burkeman, *Four Thousand Weeks*.

a lot these days. It was personal freedom or, as I call it, freedom of schedule. Freedom to determine what I want to do each day. I felt certain I could not achieve anything else on my list of intentions without first being free. My entire life plan up until now was dictated by others: parents, employers, and partners; I was not in control of my own life. I was tired of always being the responsible adult in the room. I realized this is the case for most, if not all, people in the workforce having to pay for life's expenses. But I wanted to be free and gave myself a goal to retire before I turned sixty years old. A secondary, and more important, freedom I was yearning for was freedom from my own ego. Liberation from my ego would allow my true self, the self of love and compassion, to shine through. That freedom would be a lifetime challenge to achieve.

Winter of 2019 to Winter of 2023

I was a stressed out, underslept, and overweight disaster. It was winter 2019. I put my personal physical and emotional health on the back burner. My job was eating me alive. I would sleep only five or six hours most nights and could not shut off the thoughts of work, even in my sleep. I was having shortness of breath and heart palpitations. I was coming down with colds regularly, and my face broke out with acne. I was short-tempered and would lash out at my coworkers and even those close to me.

I finally sought the advice of health professionals. The doctors referred me for stress and pulmonary tests, blood work, and an overnight sleep evaluation. All the test results came back negative. My heart and breathing were perfectly normal; in fact, my test results were all well above average. The specialists' bottom line was that I was fine physically, except for being overweight. The overnight sleep study indicated I had minor sleep apnea and insomnia. After returning to my primary care doctor, she said I was likely experiencing stress-related symptoms. My heart palpitations were anxiety attacks, likely triggered by my vagus nerve. She described the vagus nerve originating in the brain stem and extending down through the neck, chest, and abdomen. My doctor said that it could trigger increased heart rate and blood pressure from its fight-or-flight response when stressed. She recommended I lose ten to twenty pounds and address the causes of stress and improve my sleep hygiene. It was clear that I had to change direction.

My partner, or as she likes to say, my person, Katie, and I ran a farm, which compounded the work stress. During this period, we grew two acres of vegetables for our farm CSA, cultivated a greenhouse full of tomatoes in summer, harvested blueberries from a hundred bushes, sold winter greens, cut our own firewood from our woodlot, and raised a flock of sheep and a small herd of beef cows. We toiled away on the farm while we both worked full-time jobs simultaneously.

We loaded up our farmstand with beautiful, healthy vegetables each week. Our customers and neighbors stopped by to pick up their vegetables for the week and to chat with us as we scurried around putting out various farm fires. Friendly folks arrived at our farm with smiles on their faces, grateful for the healthy vegetables we grew for them, with bikes mounted on their back of cars and canoes and kayaks loaded on roof racks, heading off to mountain bike, hike a local trail, or enjoy a casual weekend paddle. We worked so hard and were losing money on top of it. We realized our farm work was providing a community service to our friends, neighbors, and customers, but we ourselves were missing out on exercise, spending time outdoors, and simply having fun.

Both my job and my farming duties were taking time away from doing what I love most: hiking, paddling, camping, attending music festivals, maintaining deep friendships, watching sunsets, and spending time with my aging dog, Quinn. I was ready to quit. To hell with my state retirement pension. The work was all-consuming, stressful, and controversial. I developed and oversaw a new statewide municipal water quality program, which put me in an uncomfortable spotlight. It was a one-person show, with me covering and visiting two hundred and fifty towns. I was responsible for extensive outreach, training, and municipal supervision. I was accountable for it all. And I needed out.

I was unwell and I had to do something. I visualized a logjam that needed to be breached. One log represented my ill physical health, the others, my emotional and mental unwellness, and my spiritual ignorance.

During this period, in the presence of Brandon and in a moment of pure spontaneous honesty, I dropped to my knees and proclaimed at the top of my lungs, "I can't do it anymore!" I could no longer be this responsible person, playing this professional role. It was a role that did not suit me, a costume I could no longer wear. I wanted to take care of myself and, most importantly, I wanted to realize my full potential. And I needed to have more fun! I had been taking life far too seriously. I began setting actionable goals to get to this place I imagined would deliver me to physical, emotional, and spiritual health. I wanted to be a better person. I wanted to help others along the way.

I knew I had to quit my job; the question was how and when. Despite my impulsive desire to quit right then and there, my pragmatic side thought I should investigate all options. After running the numbers, it seemed clear that my hard work, diligent savings, frugal spending, and not having any kids, would allow me to consider an early retirement. I was debt-free, except for my rental mortgages, and would be eligible for full Social Security in my late sixties. It's not that I would quit working entirely, but I would get to pick and choose jobs and perhaps work just part-time or seasonally. I told everyone in my circle that I wanted to take an adult gap year. My criteria for future employment or volunteer work would be that the job was stress free, and the volunteer work would be entirely rewarding.

I was excited to transition to a whole new way to "work." I had already decided I could no longer play the role of regulator and the enforcer of rules. That was just not the kind of person I was. I could no longer work in an open-office cubicle environment. I did not want to spend large chunks of my day commuting to work. I wanted to spend more time at home on my 108 acres of farm, forest, and wilderness paradise, in the place I loved, with the person I loved. I desired more free time: time to write, time to learn, time to give to others, time to travel, time to create, time to exercise, and time to be outside in nature. Little did I know, the Universe was setting the stage for an epiphany and major life change.

As Covid-19 engulfed the world, I was given the gift of time at home when all state employees transitioned to remote work. Working remotely gave me nearly two extra hours each day, simply by eliminating my commute. I could go for walks in my own woods on my lunch break or putter away at a small project. I began to see my stress levels decrease almost immediately. I fully utilized that time to help me implement my self-actualization plan. Working from home gave me a taste of what freedom might look like. I began implementing my work exit strategy so I could be fully free.

The aftershocks of the unanticipated and striking events of the deaths of Max and Lydia and collective emotion of the epic trip to Cuba (described in the previous essays in the Transformation section) left me changed and feeling like I was on a quest. But a quest for what? I was being internally guided in the direction of trying to understand the happenings. I had more questions than answers.

First, why did music have such a profound effect in all aspects of my life? Why did my quiet time next to streams, lakes, mountains, forests, stars and moon, and the sea have such a soothing and awe-inspiring impact on me? How did Brandon and I move from one intimate emotional connection to another with complete strangers in Cuba with such ease? How did others with us on our adventures feel the same emotion and deep connection during these profound and humbling shared experiences? Why did time stand still during many of my lucid happenings, and why did these events shake the ground I was walking on? How was I able to feel the imminent death of Lydia hundreds of miles away? Finally, how did the stress in my job and life impact my sleep, my weight, my skin condition, my moods, and even my organ function? I knew these important questions were somehow all linked together. I just needed to figure out their connection.

I have never thought of myself as religious, but more recently I've been thinking of myself as a spiritual person, and I would humbly describe myself as a spiritual layperson. I am only beginning this journey of understanding in reflecting over my lifetime, these principles and beliefs that have always been there, popping up from time to time as individual experiences. It turned out that the lucid experiences during this period opened a door where my spirituality awaited on the other side. The light bulb of understanding lit up as I began to align myself with Eckart Tolle's[3] definition of spirituality as the transformation of consciousness.

I began to fill my shelves with books on mindfulness, states of consciousness, quantum moments and peak experiences, Buddhism, Shamanism, Hinduism, Taoism, Druidry, Wicca, human energy fields, auras, chakras, meditation, self-actualization, Reiki, lucid dreams, synchronicity, near-death experiences, apparitions, and reincarnation. One book would lead to another, in boulder-to-boulder fashion. Some books were given to me by friends with strong recommendations that I should read them. Some had been sitting unread on my bookshelf for years but now called out to me to dive in. I started connecting the dots. I discovered that the events that occurred in the fall of 2018 through the winter of 2019 were my quantum change or peak experience, the sudden emotional and mystical happenings that caused me to hit the life reset button.

What I had previously thought of as disparate dots coalesced further, drawing a clear line, after discovering psychologist and author Dacher Keltner's 2023 book *Awe: The New Science of Everyday Wonder and How it Can Transform Your Life*.[4] Keltner identified awe as responsible for helping us feel connected to something larger than ourselves.

So much of what Keltner described matched the types of experiences I had been writing about in these pages that led to my personal awakening and transformation. Keltner stated that awe is particularly difficult to describe in words. It is ineffable. This ineffability was exactly what I was grappling with in my

---

3. Tolle, *A New Earth*.
4. Keltner, *Awe: The New Science of Everyday Wonder*.

writing about my lucid experiences. My quantum moment, also initially ineffable, kick-started my awakening to awe at a more intense level. Keltner wrote of the emotion of awe as the goosebumps that dot our arms while listening to inspiring music and the sense of wonder and mystical encounters in nature. I recounted these impactful emotions in my essay of the dramatic desert settings of Death Valley in "Saline Skies" and in the sense of place and deep connection to nature in "Judevine." He further described awe as the pathway to healing in the face of loss, growth, collaboration, and the opening of the mind. I recalled the similar sense of grief, presence, and growth after the deaths of those close to me in the essays "The Irish Wake" and "You Made a Difference" and in the forthcoming essays included in the Strange Things Happening section.

I learned that what I had been calling my collective experiences with friends and strangers (described in the essays "Saline Skies," "St. Patrick's Day 2002," "Wish I Met You Sooner," and "Angola, Cuba") were likely collective effervescence. Collective effervescence was first coined by sociologist Emile Durkheim in 1912.[5] The term refers to the sense of harmony and energy people feel when they come together in a group during a shared experience or purpose with a sense of belonging, resulting in bliss and even rapture. These writings were like a verification. It wasn't only me having these experiences. It was very satisfying to see my experiences expressed so perfectly by other authors.

I was still struggling to make sense of it all then. I needed to put my instinctual theories into practice to heal myself. I reaffirmed my commitment to yoga, Tai Chi, Qigong, regular exercise, breath work, and meditation. I became certified in Reiki and practiced self-healing daily. I attended Reiki shares regu-

---

5. Durkheim, *The Elementary Forms of Religious Life.*

larly with other certified Reiki practitioners, healing each other. I began spending days and long weekends at a local Buddhist center, honing my meditation and spiritual healing skills. I sought workshops in numerology, gemstones, essential oils, breath work, craniosacral treatments, sound healing, quantum theory, psychics, mediums, and tarot and angel cards. When I was on the table of shaman healers and Reiki masters, many of the providers said I was intuitive and had healing abilities. Sessions with mediums reaffirmed that intuitive gift. They "felt" these qualities in me. These healers also suggested I needed to heal myself before I could heal others.

I learned that my oversensitivity to people's energy and emotion described intuitive empaths. Upon entering a room, whether it's a home, a party, a concert venue or even an outdoor setting, I can immediately read the room and feel the collective energy of those in it. I began to embrace and nurture my newfound skills, but it can be a double-edged sword, as it works both in the positive and the negative. If I am not careful, I can absorb the energy and emotion of others. I am often emotionally and energetically drained after conversing with "energy vampires."

I went full in on things woo-woo. I had a deep desire to help others, family, friends, neighbors, and all those less fortunate. The gifts of humility, empathy, openness, creativity, compassion, and honesty were bestowed upon me in those initial lucid experiences. But for me to jump full bore into understanding, growing, and healing myself and others, I needed the gift of time.

Amid those transformative experiences, that initial list of life intentions had been born. I later realized I was on a journey of self-actualization,[6] finding my true self, loosening the grip of my ego, and defining why I was put on this planet, in this life. It was a journey of personal growth and development, becoming the best version of myself, and fully utilizing my talents and capabilities. I was beginning to implement my life course correction, my lucid path, as I call it. There was no going back to the old me.

While jumping onto the path of self-discovery, I was on a parallel track of writing song lyrics and, later, intense journaling. All the unexplained happenings and emotions were becoming clearer. The ineffability gap was closing. My initial lyric writing laid down the scaffolding, while the journaling and writing poured the foundation and began building the infrastructure to understanding. I started taking guitar lessons. The lessons transitioned to collaborative songwriting sessions and initial audio recordings. I reached out to my singer-songwriter friends with new lyrics. The musicians began putting music to my words. The lyrics born out of so many of these experiences were starting to come alive. This has been one of the most gratifying outcomes of my self-actualization.

Catskill Mountains, New York—March 2023

Two months after our Arctic lobster cookout event in Maine, I headed to Brandon's place to help him with his old-school one-hundred-fifty-tap maple sugaring operation, as I do each early spring. The warmer climate of the Catskill Moun-

---

6. Maslow, *Toward a Psychology of Being.*

tains allows me to have a pre-sugaring season there before I jump into Vermont's season. I always looked forward to being Brandon's sugaring assistant, collecting buckets of sap and working together feeding the wood-fired evaporator amidst the sweet steam in the sugarhouse sauna.

Brandon had previously asked me for a copy of the list of intentions I developed on that Maine trip. I had also shared with him the demo song for "4,000 Weeks." Dave Keller wrote the music and recorded the demo in one of our collaborative sessions. At the end of our sugaring weekend, the same crew from our Maine winter adventure reconvened at Brandon's place.

After two days of gathering and boiling sap, the group took a break to celebrate St. Patrick's Day at the Shire Pub in Delhi, New York. Each spring, the town hosts a St. Patrick's Day parade down the main drag in town, while high school bands and local fire departments take their turns marching in loose formations. Our group of friends had previously befriended one of the featured bagpipe bands from Schenectady. We were given VIP treatment, hanging out with the band in the pub's upstairs loft bar, downing shots and beers at band-discounted prices. The next day, sleep deprived and hungover but all smiling, the group sat me down in Brandon's living room and congratulated me for setting an early retirement date for that coming summer. My friends presented me with a piece of framed art containing two photos from our epic outing on the Maine island that January, with the list of my life intentions sandwiched between the photos. Brandon brought up the "4,000 Weeks" demo song on Leanne's phone as we all sat in silence and listened to every word. I teared up at this magnanimous gesture. It reaffirmed my retirement decision and schedule.

At the end of July 2023, after surrendering my work laptop and cell phone, I walked out the door of the five-story Montpelier headquarters of the Agency of Natural Resources one last time. It was a cleansing cutting of the umbilical cord of employment. I accomplished my first major goal in my new life course. And I was finally free!

4,000 Weeks

© Jim Ryan and Dave Keller

4,000 weeks of living
Till we face the setting sun
Into the timeless shadows
I just want to have some fun

My whole life was decided
This job is killing me
A lonely clown under the clouds
This isn't how it was meant to be

Chorus
I want to live a life that matters
Don't dismiss me out of hand
Let me see if I am the kind of man
That I think I am

Give this time here my most
I may be broke, but God I got to try
There's still so much left to do
Before I go and die

Maybe I'll go and save the world
Travel this planet and see what I might find
Find the one that got away
It all rearranged itself in my mind

Repeat chorus

Bridge
What's the worst that could happen?
What darkness holds me near?
What am I hiding from?
What is it that I fear?

4,000 weeks of living
Until we face the setting sun
Into the timeless shadows
I just want to have some fun

Scan the QR code to listen to the song,
performed by Dave Keller

STRANGE THINGS
HAPPENING

Strange Things Happening

Greenfield, Massachusetts

October 2022

I felt a pull to be with Grandpa John. Katie had work commitments she couldn't get out of, so I made the solo three-hour journey down Interstate 91 to northwestern Massachusetts. I proceeded directly to Grandpa John's house where Katie's mother, Rinky, and Aunt Debbie, and Linn, a friend and caretaker, were sitting beside him, taking turns holding his hand. Hospice was called in and they set up a hospital bed in the middle of the living room. Linn was singing him the song "We Are," by Sweet Honey in the Rock. John had been in and out of consciousness. Linn pulled me aside and shared with me that, in the last forty-eight hours, John "saw" and spoke to his mother and to his wife of sixty-plus years, Nell, both of whom had died. After reading, *The Art of Dying*,[1] a book featuring interviews with thousands of doctors, nurses, and hospice workers about what they saw and heard from the dying in their

---

1. Fenwick and Fenwick, *The Art of Dying*.

147

last days, I knew John's visions and his talking to his deceased Nell and mother were a commonplace with those near the very end. The dead were beginning to welcome and escort him to the other side.

A few days before my visit with Grandpa John, he appeared to have stabilized. He was able to get out of the hospital bed and watch a baseball game, joke, and even perform occasional dance moves on the way to the bathroom. *The Art of Dying* also describes people at the very end of their lives having moments of clarity, recalling memories, laughing, and even craving their favorite foods. At Katie's last visit with her grandfather, she told him it was "okay for him to go." John opened his eyes and said, "What the hell are you talking about?" He was as feisty as ever. So, while it appeared that he was not quite ready to leave this world just yet, he was showing symptoms of being very near the end. A few days later his condition turned.

Grandpa John's condition was deteriorating rapidly. He was ninety-four years old and until the last few months had been in relatively good health. More recently, John began having heart issues and memory problems. His sudden decline may have been attributed to a mix of morphine and pain meds, and he had been in and out of consciousness since. Debbie, John's youngest daughter, hired daily caregivers to tend to him in his home. They collectively thought he was ready to die. Katie had made a few trips there to spend time with him and to offer the family and caretakers some relief.

Grandpa John was active until near the end, especially in managing his suburban lot, meticulously mowing his lawn, edging the corners with a bread knife, planting, and tending his vegetable garden and blueberry patch by himself. When I arrived at John's house, I noticed his bed was facing the living room hallway, while behind him was a picture window facing his beloved fruit and vegetable garden. While Debbie, Linn, and I helped John sit up in bed and then transferred him to the portable commode, I suggested we spin the bed around. I wanted him to be able to face his garden and bird feeder through the large picture window, where until now, the curtains were drawn closed. The three of us spun the bed around and opened the curtains and we helped him back into the bed. John smiled at his new view.

Linn was holding Grandpa John's hand and gave up her chair for me to sit next to him. I held his hand, and he suddenly opened his eyes and said, "Who are you?" with a devilish grin. He had always joked with Katie and me that I was Katie's "special friend." Grandpa John was a very traditional Lithuanian American Catholic and often wondered out loud to Katie why I didn't yet marry her, referring to the adage "Why buy the cow when you can get the milk for free." This sexist old saying caused Katie to cringe and shake her head at her grandfather, although he never said it in front of me. When he asked, "Who are you?" it was his familiar way of playing with me. I smiled. John shook my hand and seemed grateful for my visit.

I spent the rest of that day and the next with Grandpa John, Debbie, Katie's mom, and his caretakers. He brightened up over some fun memories we had together, like making homemade horseradish in his basement; its poignancy left us both crying and laughing. The basement also served as his man space and workshop, with tools meticulously organized on the wall, and his basement kitchen, where Grandpa John loved to make homemade food and drink concoctions with recruited family members. I reminded him about making sauerkraut with his grandmother's cabbage shredder and giant wooden muddler stick. The antique three-foot-long muddler stick shed small fragments of wood into the cabbage mix that we would later have to pull out. He always sent us back to Vermont with several cases of the quart-sized mason jars that we'd offer to our farm customers, minus the splinters. It was one of our most popular items. I laughed with Grandpa John as we talked about his garden and his homemade strawberry hooch, its sweetness masking its powerful punch. After we reminisced, he fell asleep for the remaining time I was with him.

Grandpa John celebrating his ninetieth birthday (photo credit Deb Deskavich)

I needed to head home to Vermont to return to work. My thoughts continued to hover near Grandpa John in his last days. We were updated by email, text, and phone calls from Debbie. The day after I returned home, Debbie texted Katie and me that he suddenly perked up again. He wanted to get cleaned up, shaved, and dressed. Debbie and the caretakers accommodated his request. John wanted breakfast. Debbie sent us a photo of him wearing his glasses, sitting at the kitchen table fully dressed and clean-shaven. He was drinking orange juice and reading the newspaper. He was even smiling. He was having another lucid day; as it turned out, it was his final rally. Katie and I were shocked that he rebounded once again. Now it seemed like his death might not be imminent. The day after we received the photo, he again took a turn for the worse. He did not recover this time. Grandpa John died a couple of days later with Linn by his side, holding his hand.

Strange Things Happening

© Jim Ryan and Dave Keller

I got the call in the middle of the night
Jumped in the car for the three-hour drive
Made it there just before first light
For the last hour of your life

You saw visions of your mother and your wife
They were guiding you to your new life
Everything appeared so bright
And you smiled and faced the light

Pre-chorus
We sang you songs and held your hand
We turned your bed to face the land

Chorus
There were strange things happening, like I've
    never seen before
Kitchen lights flickered, and a bird flew in
    the door
I held it in my hands and it rocked me to the core
Cause I remembered what you said before

You told us right before you left
Keep your eye out, I'll be coming back
Like a red bird, I will be here
There's no need for you to shed a tear

Alternative pre-chorus

You were just saying goodbye
On your way to the other side

Repeat chorus

Bridge

I'm not sure what's next
When we leave this place
What's out there beyond
Beyond time and space

Repeat chorus

Scan the QR code to listen to the song,
performed by Carly Harvey

Whistling Up in Ghostland

Bear Swamp Farm, Vermont

Summer 2023

I was writing heartfelt emails to my closest friends, sharing my decision to take an early retirement after twenty-four years working for the State of Vermont. During a random YouTube mix of songs providing an audio backdrop to my writing endeavor, I felt like I was hit over the head by a two-by-four. Neil Young's "One of These Days" popped on. I had never heard this in my mix before. The song is about the desire to write close friends long letters from the heart. It was also one of Rita's and my favorite songs from *Harvest Moon*. That was *our* song. Rita was my aunt who had died ten months prior. A photo of her was displayed directly in front of me on my desktop shrine for a few of my recently deceased family and close friends. The song presented itself out of nowhere and descended upon me, although I've learned there are no such things as coincidences, just synchronicities. Carl Jung[1]

____

1. Jung, *Synchronicity: An Acausal Connecting Principle.*

155

described synchronicities as events carrying messages the way dreams do and providing guidance. Synchronicities provide a bridge between emotional events on the inside and those emotions outside ourselves.

I felt goosebumps dot both of my forearms, making those hairs stand up straight, and a tingling sensation filled my body. I sobbed, the tears coming from a place deep within. It was a cleansing cry, a cathartic one, a cry that felt needed and felt good. It was one in a series of cathartic cries since the profound events in the fall and winter of 2018–2019 (described in the Transformation section). I felt Rita's presence for the first time since she died. The effect of the unexpected visit was immediate and intense. She was with me, around me, inside of me.

In the early summer of 2023, I was in two worlds. One was a world of stress related to quitting my job to take an early retirement. An enormous workload was piled upon me in the last few weeks of my employment. As I was wrapping up my tenure and training my replacement, an unexpected and catastrophic flood hit Vermont. During my career with the state, I had often been mobilized to assist in flood recovery work. For my last three weeks working for the state, I tasked myself with determining what caused the extensive flood damage to Vermont's town roads, culverts, and bridges, what I called flood forensics. I thought we could learn from the causes of past flooding to better prepare for the next catastrophic event. It was stressful, yet necessary and fulfilling work, a chance to make one last contribution before my departure.

Simultaneously, I was fully immersed in my second world, this one more creative and personally revealing in nature. I was preparing for the release of my collaborative album *Free Now*. I was navigating the unknown territory of self-promotion, nervous about hosting an album release concert, distributing the album, writing and distributing press releases, and doing on-air radio interviews both on my own and with the musicians on the album. This quiet introvert was making his creative debut, alongside some very talented musicians. I was the behind-the-scenes lyricist; after all, the musicians would be the ones doing the actual performing, but I was terrified, nonetheless.

During this period of intense work, creativity, and preparation, it seemed like a mystic firehose of happenings was occurring all around me. The album was being played on five different local radio stations; three of them featured the album in special local spotlight programs. My friends and neighbors were emailing and calling, saying they heard my songs on the radio. People around me said I was sparking energetically. A lifelong dream of making an album of my song lyrics came to fruition. And to top it off, my goal of taking an early retirement was being realized simultaneously. As positive as it all was, it was completely nerve-racking. I realized the wisdom in the adage "Be careful what you wish for!"

Rita was one of my closest and favorite relatives, like a second mom, or even a big sister. She was only fifteen years older than I was. But she always loved to remind me that she had changed my diapers as my teenage babysitter. Rita and my uncle, Billy, visited us often from Connecticut for the Vermont fall foliage season or for his favorite activity, bass fishing on nearby ponds. We also hosted my family Thanksgiving holiday together for several years at our farm. Rita and Billy brought all the fixings for the perfect Bloody Mary mix and assigned me as the alchemist. After a couple of stiff drinks, my cousin Kristy, Rita and Billy's daughter, played DJ with the Spotify mix on her phone, while Rita sang along. The holiday gathering transitioned into an impromptu dance party, as my mother, Rita's sister, and the rest of the family crew pushed the furniture against the walls to make room for the hip swinging in the living room.

Rita died in August 2022 after a ten-year struggle with Parkinson's disease and a series of small strokes. I watched her slowly diminish over that time from a carefree, fun, and always laughing person to one who could no longer care for herself. My seventy-nine-year-old Uncle Billy was her 24/7 caretaker.

I was with her for the last days of her life in the hospital in Bridgeport, Connecticut, along with Billy, Kristy, my brother Chris, my mother, and my stepfather, Steve. Although her health diminishment was a slow slog, the end came unexpectedly and suddenly. We took turns sitting with Rita around the clock. We didn't want her to die alone in the hospital. My brother Chris, my cousin Kristy, and I softly played some of her favorite songs and musicians, including Neil Young and the moving song "Fare Thee Well" by Marcus Mumford and Oscar Isaac. The latter was the same song that shook me on the drive back from my friend Max's Irish wake (described in "The Irish Wake" essay). We sat with her, held her hand, caressed her skin, and brushed her hair. I whispered in her ear that I loved her, saying it was okay for her to go, and asked her to visit me when she made it to the other side. Rita had been unresponsive since entering the hospital, but several in the room, including me, saw Rita begin to twitch her legs and arms and move her lips while I was whispering in her ear. It was as though she was trying to speak but couldn't get the words out or open her eyes. I was in the room when she drew her last breath, holding her hand. That was the first time in my life someone died in my presence.

Rita Gerdo (photo credit Gerard Costantino)

Back alone at my desk, trying to process Rita's "visit" moments before, I was interrupted by Katie popping her head in the room to say dinner was ready. My uncharacteristic reply was, "I won't be eating dinner tonight." After a double take from Katie, I added, "Rita just visited me." Katie understood. She knew I was a conduit for the dead to visit. Her reply was a matter-of-fact, "Okay," and she shut the office door and gave me my space to be with Rita.

I was compelled to write a song on the spot about this happening to help me process what unfolded. It was the birth of "Whistling Up in Ghostland." The power of music was reaffirmed yet again. Certain songs have the ability to stop me in my tracks and change my state of consciousness and therefore a core component of my spirituality. When this happens, I put aside whatever I am doing, so I can focus on the events as they occur. I enter a state of deep awareness. This was a pattern for me: a lucid experience starting with a consciousness shift, a slap in the face to the everyday, an expulsion of my ego, an awakening, and a deep sense of presence and clarity.

Author and medium Mark Anthony's book *The Afterlife Frequency*[2] helped me understand why I was able to communicate with the dead. Anthony described matter, emotion, and thoughts as forms of energy. All energy vibrates at different frequencies. Through his research of quantum physics, human brainwave activity monitoring, and interviews of those that have survived near death experiences, Anthony stated that people who meditate regularly, spend time in nature, are empathetic and self-aware, and are fully present vibrate at higher frequencies. When you vibrate at a higher frequency it allows you to be more aligned and receptive with those on the other side, because spirits also vibrate at a higher frequency. He wrote that communication with the dead was "interdimensional communication," and this conveyance often occurred during sleep visitations, premonitions, shared death experiences, and synchronicities. Anthony developed the term "electromagnetic soul" and uses it interchangeably with the terms "life force," "soul," and "consciousness." Anthony, and many other authors and scientists, believe that the soul is preexistent to the body and survives after the human body dies. It is eternal energy that never dies. I was now coming to terms with this in my spiritual and intuitive awakening.

Rita only wanted to say hello to me, or at least that's what

---

2. Anthony, *The Afterlife Frequency*.

it felt like. She wanted to say she was okay being on the other side. I had asked her to visit me, and she did; it just took a bit longer than I thought. Rita's visit was not the first, nor will it be the last. I sometimes feel like I am a bus stop for the dead as they pass through on their ride to their final destination. Various deceased relatives and friends have let me know of their presence, usually through my dreams, on their way to the other side.

Sometimes when I am driving in my car with the radio on, thinking about one of my close friends or family members who has died, a song connected to that person will suddenly fill the car. I can summon the dead when I am in the right frame of mind by playing songs with a connection to the person. This happens most often when I am in an outdoor setting, like sitting on my back porch just before sunset. In these spaces and in that state of mind, I attempt to conjure up a visit. Most of *my dead* feel compelled to come in on songs, *their* songs, or *our* songs.

Ghostland is an intentionally created sacred place located on my friend Brandon's mountaintop meadow in the Catskill Mountains. The center of the two-acre meadow is adorned with a large metal Celtic cross and stone-ringed hearth, surrounded by fluttering Tibetan peace flags and eight home-made "Live the Sun" flags fifteen feet high and fastened to hardwood pole trees. A towering wood sculpture located on the far end of the meadow sits on its own platform with a ten-foot-wide diameter sun and sun rays projecting out another ten feet facing the fire circle. The orange sun sculpture is painted with the mantras "Live the Sun" on the top and "Black Water" on the bottom of its circle, honoring the goddesses of sunlight and the darkness of the Adirondack waters. The name Ghostland was bestowed upon this special place by Brandon, Leanne, and Joe on the drive home from an Albany concert by the band The Ghost of Paul Revere. That band emotionally connected the three on that concert outing as a close-knit group, calling themselves the Ghost Riders, which John and I would later join. Ghostland became a place for friends to gather to play music, read poetry, build epic wood sculptures, burn colossal bonfires, perform bizarre theatrical acts, set intentions, perform Earth-based spiritual ceremonies, host Mountain Jam festivals, and share positive energies with like-minded souls. It was at one of the Mountain Jam festivals where Brandon and Leanne first fell in love.

Ghostland (photo credit Brandon Dennis)

I was fascinated with the prospect that I would be able to visit my friends when I died and journeyed to the other side, in a place like Ghostland, by riding in on a song. It became the centerpiece for my lyrics in "Whistling Up in Ghostland."

Someday, when a song that connected me to my friends pops on seemingly at random, or perhaps when they are thinking about me in synchronistic fashion, they will know it is me paying them a visit to let them know that I am okay.

Whistling Up in Ghostland

© Jim Ryan

Sometimes I feel them in the wind
I see their faces in the clouds
I talk to them in my dreams
I often cry out loud

Why do the dead visit me?
I'm not really afraid
They're the stars that paint the night
The rising sun at the start of day

Chorus
When I'm whistling up in Ghostland
In that new place where I belong
I will join Heaven's band
And I'll ride in on a song

After I'm gone, I'll still be around
I'll flow with the waterfalls
I will be the rain upon your face
We're all just energy after all

Repeat Chorus

Someday they'll feel me in the wind
They will see my face in the clouds
They will talk to me in their dreams
And they will cry out loud

I Just Lost a Good Friend Today
Lamoille River Valley, Vermont

February 2024

Sean came home from Mass General on Thursday afternoon. He arrived to find a hospital bed in his living room, where the recliner once stood, and in the hallway, a walker, a wheelchair, and a portable commode. These essential items were evidence that Lamoille Home Health and Hospice had arrived in his home and foretold what Sean's immediate future would look like. I stopped by later that afternoon, after checking in with Sean's wife, Nancy, to make sure that my visit would be okay. Sean was awake and lucid, watching CNN. He greeted me with a softer than normal, gravelly voice, "Jimmy," a nickname I haven't used since high school. Sean liked to add the letter *y* to random things and people. I, in turn, nicknamed him Seany. He reached out for a handshake and asked, "How do I look?" Always one to give and appreciate brutal honesty, he told me not to lie in my response. I said, "Sean, you look like shit." I told him he had lost a lot of weight and looked weak. He just nodded his head, saddened, but grateful for the honest answer.

Sean's health was declining rapidly from the cancer ravaging his entire body. In January 2014 Sean was diagnosed with metastatic pancreatic neuroendocrine tumors. Doctors found the cancer by accident during an emergency room visit for gallstones. By the time the cancer was discovered, it had spread throughout his body. If there was any good news about the malignant cancer diagnosis, it was that it was slow growing. Sean was placed in a clinical trial at Dana-Farber Cancer Institute in Boston soon after. That experimental treatment kept his cancer at bay for many years, until then.

Sean had been in and out of Copley Hospital in nearby Morrisville, in pain, bloated with fluids, and weak. His doctors decided he should be moved to Mass General in Boston, where he would stay for a week to rest, drain fluids, and decide next steps. After first offering a new type of chemotherapy as an alternative, the doctors then decided it was too risky to receive the treatment, which promised minimal benefit. Instead, his oncologists delivered him the prognosis. He had two to three months to live. After valiantly battling cancer for ten years, Sean finally decided to stop fighting.

Since the initial diagnosis in 2014, Sean aggressively fought the cancer and went on with his life. In winter, he was employed full-time on ski patrol, skiing nearly one hundred days each season. In summer, he worked full-time on their vegetable farm, tinkered on his antique British MG cars, rode his BMW motorcycle, and sailed.

On that day, when visiting Sean at his hospice-equipped home, I began asking him what he would like the coming days and weeks to look like. Who did he want to see and what did he want to do or talk about when he was feeling up to it? I was honored when Sean included me, his ski patrol buddy Wayne, and our partners among the only people he wanted to be there every day, in addition to Nancy, his stepson, Andrew, and Sean's immediate family. He suggested he would like short visits with small groups of people. I told him he could tell me to "Go the fuck home" when he was tired of me. He said, "Don't worry, I will." Sean never liked to sugarcoat his words. One thing on his to-do list was visiting his ski patrol friends at Smugglers' Notch. He also said he'd like to go for a ride. When I asked where he wanted to go, he said, "It doesn't matter." That made me kind of sad, until he added that maybe we could go to the drive-through window of a fast food joint and order a chocolate milkshake, despite his lack of appetite.

Nancy entered the living room as I sat with Sean. She began recalling Sean's fishing stories and spoke of their trip last summer to Gloucester, where Sean pointed out the boats he had captained at the local dock. She shared photos of Sean standing in front of his boats. When Nancy left the room, I told Sean I would sit with him, talk to him, or even play music for him, depending on how he was feeling. I said I hoped he knew he could talk to me about anything. I mentioned I was spiritual but not religious in the Christian sense. Sean reminded me he was a born-again Christian, that he had accepted Christ through one of his born-again friends twenty years ago and he would be welcomed in heaven. Although I probably knew this at one time, I was taken aback. The Sean I knew and loved was a foul-mouthed commercial fishing captain turned vegetable farmer with a love for telling off-color and politically incorrect jokes that seemed equally offensive to all. But everyone who knew him appreciated his kind heart and his willingness to do most anything for those close to him.

Sean said he was not afraid of death. I shared with him that the dead often visit me in my dreams and even during the day. I described several books I had recently read about what happens to people near and at death, many of whom have the shared experiences of seeing a bright, warm light, being welcomed by deceased relatives and spouses, and feeling deep love and compassion. Sean nodded his head but said he had not come home to die, changing his tune from the prior day. He thought if he got his kidney and liver strength back up, the doctors could perform another radiation treatment or two. He had proven his doctors wrong in the past and he would do so again, even facing this dire prognosis. Sean was always a fighter. It was difficult for him to surrender to what amounted to his death sentence.

Two days later, his buddy Wayne got Sean into his car and took him up to visit their ski patrol buddies. Sean and Wayne found each other late in life when Sean joined ski patrol well into his fifties. The two of them hit it off immediately during the tough yet fulfilling days and fun times in the ski patrol shack on the mountain. During breaks, they enjoyed the camaraderie with the guys and women on patrol. Sean had many friends growing up in New Hampshire and Maine whom he continued to stay in touch with, but Wayne and Sean were best friends in the last years of Sean's life.

On a rare sunny afternoon during the several-weeks-long stretch of mid-winter cloudy days, Wayne and Lynne succeeded in getting Sean to Smugglers' Notch. At Sean's request, Wayne wheeled Sean in before the patrollers arrived and set him up on a bench and then removed the wheelchair from view. Sean was extremely proud and didn't want his buddies to see him in his uncharacteristically feeble condition. Sean was welcomed warmly by the ski patrol crew who had just finished their shift. At Sean's request, Wayne had brought a bottle of high-end whiskey to pass around during the visit. After the ski patrol crew left, Wayne and his wife Lynne got him back into the car, where he put the seatback down and immediately fell asleep for the forty-five-minute drive home. They were all exhausted. Wayne and Lynn struggled to get Sean into the house, dodging patches of ice in the driveway. They helped him out of his clothes and assisted him into the hospital bed. He joked with Wayne in very Sean-like fashion to "Watch your hands" as Wayne helped him get undressed. We all appreciated Sean's unique and unfiltered sense of humor, even in his final days.

Sean's condition deteriorated significantly in the coming days. He was barely eating and began hallucinating and talking to himself. Or was he? Perhaps he, like the handful of my recently departed friends and family in their last days, was talking to those on the other side? His hospice doctor visited and updated his prognosis: The end would come in a matter of days. Lynne drove to my house to go over Sean's care coverage to be divided among the four of us: Lynne, Wayne, Katie, and me. We planned out the month of February, knowing in all likelihood it wouldn't be that long. One of us would be responsible for checking in with Nancy to relieve her and would spend time with Sean each day. We were all taking things one day at a time.

Aside from the official care schedule, I stopped at Sean and Nancy's house nearly every day while he was on hospice to give Nancy a hug, help her with whatever tasks needed doing, talk to her, and just listen to her vent about the current situation. I sat with Sean and talked to him; sometimes he responded and sometimes not. I downloaded some of Sean's favorite music onto my phone: John Prine, Aretha Franklin, Delbert McClinton, Traffic, Little Feat, Creedence Clearwater Revival, and big band swing music. I played the music when Sean and I were alone. When he was awake, I always asked him before playing the music in case he didn't feel up to it. His response was always yes.

Nancy told me one recent night Sean tried to get out of bed to use the bathroom, but he was not strong enough. Nancy and the hospice staff feared that if Sean attempted to walk, he would fall and hurt himself. Breaking a bone at this stage of Sean's illness could have been catastrophic. Nancy pivoted to me as I sat next to Sean and said, "Jim, I need you to stay on the couch tonight." Nancy had gotten very good at asking for help, after her close group of friends, including me, asked her to do just that. Between spending hours with Sean and dealing with family coming from New Hampshire and Maine, Nancy said she was physically and emotionally exhausted. I said I would be glad to stay the night. We agreed I would head home for a couple of hours to grab my overnight stuff and have dinner with Katie and come back in the evening. I walked over to Sean and put my hand on his arm and told him I had to leave. Sean, having a lucid moment, grabbed my hand and shook it as firmly as he could. He said to me, "Thank you for being here with me." I said I was glad to be here and that I would be coming back to be his roommate tonight. He gave me the thumb wave, which indicated, "Get the hell out of here." I laughed all the way to the car.

The normal fifteen-minute drive from Sean's house to my place took nearly double that time as the forty-degree temperatures thawed our gravel roads and turned them into soupy, rutted mud. The worst section of the road was several hundred feet before my driveway. I pulled into our dooryard exhausted, greeted by Katie and our shelter mutt, Quinn. They both seemed to empathize with my condition. I updated Katie on the latest happenings at Sean and Nancy's and told her I would be staying overnight with Sean. Katie suggested I take a nap.

I grabbed my dog-eared copy of *The Art of Dying*[1] and my reading glasses, and headed to the couch, with Quinn on the floor beside me as I stroked her. I had been rereading *The Art of Dying* and *Surviving Death*[2] by Leslie Kean to help me understand Sean's transition from life to death. I found both books helpful in understanding what happens to people near death from the perspective of the dying person's family and the doctors, nurses, and hospice workers who are near them during this time.

Settled on the couch, I found myself falling asleep. I was in that half-asleep, half-awake state when I entered the strangest dreamlike scene. I was back at Sean and Nancy's house, sitting on the couch directly across from Sean in his hospital bed. He was "talking" to me, but it wasn't Sean in his current nearly nonverbal and physically immobile condition. It was the healthy, vibrant Sean, known to me before this recent rapid decline. The healthier version of Sean was lying on his side facing me, wearing his regular eyeglasses, which he hadn't been wearing of late. His head propped up on his bent elbow, he was "telling" me how hard this dying was on him but almost casually, how it really sucked, and how weak he felt. He even said all the visitors were too much for him. In Sean's communication

---

1. Fenwick and Fenwick, *The Art of Dying*.
2. Kean, *Surviving Death*.

with me, his lips did not move. It was as if it was telepathic communication, from his consciousness to mine. My eyes popped open as I was jarred awake, until I remembered I was on my couch at home.

Trying to tell Katie about the exchange Sean and I had before I left his house, his heartfelt thank you to me, I couldn't finish my sentence. I felt deep compassion for what he was going through, and Sean's gratitude to me in that moment meant the world to me as my eyes filled with tears and I began to shake. I had never really cried in front of Katie in our thirteen-plus years together. With her arms around me, I knew I could let it all out, and I did just that. I pulled myself together, showered, grabbed my stuff, and headed back to be with Sean.

Nancy was relieved that I was staying overnight. She had refilled her coffee mug full of Chardonnay on ice and sat in the recliner next to Sean as I grabbed a seat on the couch next to Woody, their pit bull mix. Nancy said she appreciated being able to enjoy some wine and could relax now that I was there. I pulled out my phone and played some music, the Bluegrass Gospel Project. It was one of Nancy's favorite Vermont bands; she and I saw them play together live several times before they disbanded. Nancy needed some comforting music and a distraction, and my choice was for her.

Nancy wove in and out of crying and laughing about how hard this current situation was, and how difficult it had been over Sean's ten-year struggle with cancer, but she smiled as she reminisced about how much fun they had together. This was Nancy's second stint as a full-time caretaker, since she took daily care of Andrew after his ATV accident, in which he suffered a traumatic brain injury and has been wheelchair bound ever since. Andrew's strength, compassion, and sense of humor, despite his physical condition, kept her grounded and in awe. For more than a decade Andrew transitioned from living with his mom to living with round-the-clock roommates in separate housing, but he stayed with Sean and Nancy alternate weekends. He would be arriving the next day with his caregiver. Andrew hadn't seen Sean in weeks because of recent hospital stays. Andrew and Sean had always been very close. Sean helped care for Andrew and fully incorporated Andrew into his life, and their lives on the farm. In true Sean fashion, the two would howl at Sean's inappropriate jokes about Andrew's disability, with Andrew laughing even harder than Sean. They would take Andrew everywhere in his accessible van, they purchased a wheelchair with tracks for Andrew to be able to ride around the farm, and Sean even adapted his fishing boat so it could accommodate Andrew's wheelchair.

Nancy wept when she recalled the memory of Sean once telling her, "Andrew has made me be a better person." It was so true. Because of Sean's time with Andrew, Sean volunteered for the Vermont Adaptive Ski and Sports program and the Special Olympics, assisting people with disabilities so they could ski down mountains, tethered to their volunteer helpers. Sean absolutely loved that job, and the disabled people in that program adored Sean, some becoming lifelong friends. Sean became especially close with one client in the Vermont adaptive ski program. Jacob and his parents drove to Vermont from Delaware so he could ski with Sean. Even after Sean transitioned from the adaptive ski program to working full-time with ski patrol, Sean would take a week off from patrol just to ski with his young friend. His parents never forgot Sean's kindness to their son. They became very close with Sean and Nancy and still come up to Vermont each summer to spend a week working hard on their farm to help in any way they can.

Nancy refilled her coffee cup with white wine a few more times while we sat and reminisced, before she headed up the steps to bed, followed shortly by Woody. I was relieved I wouldn't be sharing the couch with the dog. After all, the couch was Woody's larger-than-life dog bed, full of his and the cat, Mikey's, hair. I picked up a whodunit paperback for a mindless distraction before turning in. The couch was about four feet away from Sean's hospital bed. I heard Sean struggle to breathe throughout the night, as I fell in and out of sleep. Sean's breathing sounded like a person with severe sleep apnea. There were very long pauses in between breaths, multiple seconds. It scared me, as I thought he had stopped breathing altogether several times throughout the night.

Nancy set up a baby monitor and listened attentively, equally concerned, from her bedroom upstairs. She came down a few times during the night to check on Sean. After a fitful night, I again came to a half-awake, half-asleep state. It was almost identical to what had happened to me earlier that after-noon on my couch at home. Twice in one day, the "old Sean" had come to visit and speak to me. He was again lying in the hospital bed, facing me, "talking" to me, again without moving his lips. This time Sean was sharing how his breathing was becoming more difficult. He didn't like all the people fussing over him, bathing him, moving him, helping him go to the bathroom. After this "conversation," I was again jolted fully awake.

In recent years, I felt I had the ability to communicate with those on the other side. This was only the second time someone still alive, but nonverbal and near death, communi-cated with me. My previous experience was the moment of clairsentience, where I felt pain in my sternum while fully awake, indicating Lydia's passing shortly before it occurred several hundred miles away (described in the "You Made a Difference" essay). Mark Anthony[3] describes the solar plexus, located just below the sternum, as the second brain due to the vast number of nerve fibers and where we receive messages of emotional sensory and intuition. With these two communications with Sean, it was more telepathic in nature, a visual and verbal communication, more than a sensory one, in a dreamlike state. I later read that the edges of sleep are ripe for consciousness change, as the ego begins its slumber and the portal to lucid dreaming and intuitive happenings opens.[4] Anthony described these experiences as "shared death experiences," that the experience is shared by the dying and those caring for them, an "interdimensional communication." I looked over at him from the couch and wondered if that lucid Sean was somewhere inside of him right then, despite his physical condition.

Wayne stayed with Sean Saturday night. He sat in the chair all night and didn't sleep. Before Nancy turned in, she and Wayne sat up talking, reminiscing, and crying. Katie and I ventured over the next day on our deeply rutted swampy roads. The house was full of Sean and Nancy's people, coming and going all day Sunday.

Most of the visitors were sitting around the kitchen table eating, drinking, and conversing. Candice, Sean's ex-wife and mother of his two daughters, brought some old photo albums

---

3. Anthony, *The Afterlife Frequency*.
4. Dumpert, *Liminal Dreaming*.

from Sean's days in high school. Sean and Candice were high school sweethearts. She also brought some photos of Sean's early days fishing. Sean was born in Maine and his family moved to Littleton, New Hampshire, when he was young. Sean and his brother spent summers on Bailey Island off the coast of Maine, where Sean's love of the sea was born. He began as a fishing boat hand as a teenager, and in his mid-twenties became a commercial fishing captain out of Portland, Gloucester, and Boston. Sean and his crew were fishing two hundred miles from shore in Georges Bank during the infamous October 1991 storm, detailed in the *Perfect Storm* bestseller and movie. Sean and his crew made it back to port safely, after navigating the roughest seas he had ever encountered. Shortly after Sean met Nancy, he gave up his fishing career to be with Nancy and to try his hand at vegetable farming. I met Sean for the first time shortly after he started dating Nancy. He eventually moved to Nancy's place to start up the farm together.

Bouquets of flowers brought by the visitors filled the corners of the kitchen and the living room. Visitors also brought a variety of foods: mini-cheesecakes, pulled pork from Sean and Nancy's pigs, homemade coffee cake, lasagna, quiche, and organic shade-grown coffee. The latter I knew wasn't Sean's coffee, since he preferred the less fancy Folgers or Maxwell House from his fishing boat days.

I swooped in to take advantage of a moment of audio lull to pull out my cell phone and play what I thought would be appropriate music for Sean in his current condition. I had previously downloaded the "John Prine's Greatest Hits" playlist from Spotify. The first song up was "Angel from Montgomery," two versions, John Prine's original and a duet version with John and Bonnie Raitt. I began to well up, as Sean's eyes opened for a brief second. Sean's eyebrows rose and he perked up. I leaned in and whispered, "It's Jimmy here, and I wanted to play your favorite musician." I admitted John Prine was one of my favorite lyricists and thanked Sean for turning me on to him years prior.

Katie came to my side when she saw the tears in my eyes. Next out of the Spotify gate was "Clay Pigeons." That song, even more than "Angel from Montgomery" hit a deep emotional nerve with me. This time I cried even harder, my face falling into my hands on my lap. Katie came back over to comfort me and rub my back. I continued to weep as the sound of laughter from the visitors wafted in from the kitchen next door. Katie alerted me that Sean's eyes were open and his facial expression had changed. I continued to play more John Prine and moved the phone beside Sean's ear, at Katie's suggestion. John Prine's classically funny "Fish and Whistle," a song I always loved, seemed so appropriate now, the story song about whistling and going fishing in heaven. The visualization of Sean whistling up in heaven fishing, inspired the song, essay, and book title "Whistling Up in Ghostland," with Ghostland representing heaven. I imagined Sean laughing at that line if he could.

The visitors in the kitchen began transitioning into the living room, joining me as I sat with Sean, and Katie returned to the kitchen to spend some time with Nancy. One of the guests turned on the Super Bowl on the very large flat-screen TV. It was the same room in which Sean was lying only a few feet away. It was a surreal juxtaposition: Super Bowl partiers cheering the football action and assessing the game's commercials, while Sean lay in his hospital bed with labored breathing and occasional moans of discomfort. At times that evening I struggled. I couldn't shake the familiar feeling of incongruity with the simultaneous happenings occurring in the same room. I kept reliving the Super Bowl party in the very same house the night Lydia passed almost five years ago to the day (described in the "You Made a Difference" essay) and that same sense of incongruity on that night.

Nancy returned to the living room and attempted to give Sean some liquid pain meds applied with a syringe down his throat. Sean reacted with nonstop deep hacking. Katie and I assisted Nancy in trying to calm him down and reposition him to stop the coughing. The coughing fit finally passed. As soon as Sean calmed down, I pulled Katie aside and said we should head home for a brief reprieve. Nancy had already asked either Katie or me to stay the night again. I told Nancy we would both be spending the night, but we had to let our dog Quinn out and grab our overnight stuff.

After another slow and nearly perilous mud-rutted drive home and a quick Quinny walk in the backyard, we headed back after grabbing some sheets, pillows, and books to read. Poor Quinny seemed shocked that we were both leaving so soon, as she was almost never left overnight by herself. We arrived back at Nancy's at nearly 10:00 that night. The game would be going into overtime, a rarity for the Super Bowl. I rolled my eyes and muttered, "Great!" I knew we would be going to bed late, as the remaining visitors watched the rest of the game.

Katie and I finally settled in well after midnight. Katie grabbed Woody's couch, and I lounged awkwardly in the recliner. We both read for an hour or so before turning off the lights. Katie fell asleep quickly. I was in my head, trying to lull myself to sleep with the rhythmic whooshing of Andrew's BiPAP machine in the next room, which he used since his traumatic brain injury. The regular humming and hissing of the machine could not lull me to sleep as I had hoped. I finally fell into a light doze after 2:00 in the morning, napping in and out, waking nearly every time Sean's breathing halted, until 6:00.

Two days later, I headed to the sugar woods. My friends Jim and Michael and I had begun a new maple sugaring partnership using Michael's existing sugarhouse, equipment, and sugarbush. On that Tuesday, we had been replacing drop lines and tapping trees for an hour and a half before Michael, a dedicated writer, had to peel off to get ready for an appointment with a writing consultant. Michael checked his watch: 1:35. He was running late. Minutes after he left, the sun broke through the clouds in spectacular fashion, after weeks of almost total cloudiness. I remarked on the sun's reappearance to Jim and said how lucky we were to be tapping in sunshine with no wind on this beautiful day, especially after we got soaked the weekend before. Jim and I worked together for a couple more hours before I said I had to head out to be with Sean.

I gathered up my gear and snowshoed out of the woods a quarter mile to Michael's house and my car. I checked my cell phone in his driveway, unsure if I would have coverage. I was in the habit of seeing if there were any Sean updates. There were. A text from Katie let me know that Sean had passed at 1:40. I wasn't surprised at the timing. I had just confided in Michael before we headed out to the woods that I thought Sean was going to die on that day, after he had asked me about Sean's condition. That expectation did not relieve the blow I had just been given. I later pieced together that Sean had died at almost the exact moment the spectacular sunshine arrived in the sugar woods.

Katie's text went on to say that Nancy had sequestered herself in her greenhouse, where her one hundred laying hens were housed, so she could avoid seeing Sean's now lifeless body lying in her living room, awaiting the pickup by the crematorium. We later learned it took the crematorium nearly three hours to arrive. It probably felt like a lot longer to her. Katie said Nancy chose to be alone but would want company later that evening. I texted Katie to say I was on my way home. I put on Sean's Aretha Franklin CD for the twenty-minute drive home. The tears came even before I turned the key and continued as I pulled into my driveway, parked the car, and turned off the ignition, still listening to Aretha. Katie let Quinn out onto the front porch, where she waited for me to come in to greet her as I normally do. I finished out the song, gathered up my maple sugaring gear and headed in, attempting to wipe the tears from my eyes. I dropped my snowshoes in the mudroom and kicked off my slip-on muck boots.

Katie gave me a hug and asked how I was dealing with the news about Sean. I said I was both sad and relieved at that moment. For Katie, it was more of a gut punch. That image struck me, and I realized my response to Katie hadn't done justice to how I really felt. I too felt gut punched and brought to my knees. I started to cry, again, while we were hugging. I hadn't been drinking very much in recent days but, on this day, I planned on getting sauced. I grabbed a beer. I headed to my office with my cell phone, laptop, and portable speaker. I needed to hear Sean's songs, the playlist I put together for his wedding with Nancy, The Clash's *London Calling* double album I had played for him on our last ride home from Mass General that Sean sang and I banged on the steering wheel to, and the tunes I played for him softly at his bedside in his nearly two weeks in hospice.

I surrendered into the sobbing as I went deeper into Sean's music library. I began making a specific Sean playlist and cranked the music loud. I grabbed my songwriting notebook and jotted down new song lyrics as I played the music. The first beer went down fast, and I headed into the kitchen for another. This time I also reached for an un-opened bottle of maple bourbon I'd received as a Christmas gift and poured two short glasses for Katie and me, neat. Katie was cooking in the kitchen, her way of coping, as I was making music lists and writing lyrics influenced by Sean. I wrote three songs inspired by Sean in the days immediately before, during, and after his death. The songs helped me to process my grief and the strange happenings of my half-awake, half-asleep states and to honor Sean.

I got through a couple dozen Sean songs in the new playlist, since I knew Nancy would put me in charge of the music after Sean's service. Katie asked if I wanted to go with her back to Nancy's place or if I wanted to stay home and continue listening to music. I said I wanted to go with her to be with Nancy but couldn't drive; I already had a good buzz on. I showered and slipped on more comfortable clothes, before jumping into Katie's Tacoma truck.

Andrew, Nancy, her nephew Jeffrey, Wayne, Lynne, and Sean's sister, Mary Francis, were all in the kitchen when I arrived there hours after Sean's death. All, except Jeffrey, had been with Sean, holding and touching Sean or each other as he took his last breath. Sean's other sister, Cathy, from New Hampshire, was also there when Sean died but she headed home shortly after Sean died. Wayne shared with us that they had the local country radio station, WLVB, playing on Sean's last day. At the exact moment of Sean's death, John Prine's song "Spanish Pipedream" suddenly and strangely presented itself. It was Sean's favorite song. After I looked at the lyrics, I understood why. It is a song about a topless dancer who had something up her sleeve, giving life advice to the narrator about throwing out your TV, going to the country, having a garden, eating peaches, and having kids. I told the group gathered at Nancy's house I was going to call WLVB the next morning and dedicate that same song to Sean. The group reminisced about Sean's fishing days and Nancy's plans for his celebration of life as Jeffrey and I sipped honey-flavored Jim Beam. Everyone was sleep-deprived and emotionally spent.

I broke down, bawling on the phone with the DJ the next morning when making the song request, as he patiently waited for me to gather myself and get my words out. The DJ played the song a few minutes later, with Nancy, Andrew, and Wayne listening. Sean went out with his favorite song playing as his friends and family clustered over him. I wanted to dedicate that song to Sean again, this time to wish him well on his journey.

About a month and a half after Sean passed, Katie and I helped Nancy and her friends and family prepare for Sean's celebration of life service at the Nazarene Church in Johnson. Katie baked what seemed like enough lemon cookies for one hundred people. The service attendees converged an hour before the service in the church basement, bringing cheese platters, pastries, fruit dishes, coffee, and cider. We set up chairs and tables and an ongoing laptop reel of electronic photos of

Sean skiing, farming, fishing, and hanging out with friends. I set up my portable speaker with my cell phone nearby to play the Spotify mix of Sean's favorite songs.

The service began at 1:00, and the church began to fill long beforehand. The Smugglers' Notch ski patrollers were there in force. Several dozen showed up in their red parkas emblazoned with white crosses. After welcoming words and some scripture readings, the pastor talked about Sean. He shared stories about Sean being born in Rumford, Maine, and moving to Littleton, New Hampshire, his love of skiing that began at age four, his summers on Bailey Island outside Portland, Maine, his fishing and captaining days in Portland, Boston, and Gloucester, how he met Nancy with the assistance of online dating, his transition to farming, and becoming a ski patroller. The pastor spoke about Sean's special relationship with Andrew and his work with the disabled in the adaptive ski program. He acknowledged Sean's love of music, especially John Prine, and played three of the artist's songs during the service: "Beautiful World," "How Lucky Can One Man Get," and of course, "Spanish Pipedream," the song played on the radio in synchronicity with Sean's death. I had never heard "Beautiful World" before. It was especially poignant and emotionally impactful at that moment.

Many in attendance got up and spoke into the microphone, as it was passing around the room. Sean's friends and family shared stories about his love of being on ski patrol, of how he made deep friendships with the parents of one of the disabled children, about his love of storytelling, dirty jokes, and profanities. They spoke of Sean's lack of farming experience and how he became a knowledgeable and respected farmer. I mustered up the emotional courage to recite the song lyrics I wrote on the day Sean died. It was a shortened version of what became the lyrics for "I Just Lost a Good Friend Today." I skipped some additional stories I wanted to tell about my time in the car with Sean taking him back and forth to Sean's cancer treatments in Boston. I didn't want to lose it in front of the group. I mostly held it together.

Most attending the service adjourned to the basement for the fellowship celebration. I shared several big hugs with Nancy; she had been very nervous and overwhelmed, leading up to the event. I told her she'd done great and the hard part of the service was now over. She seemed relieved and reminded me I needed to make a large batch of Bloody Marys for Saturday. That was the day fifty-plus ski patrollers and many of Sean's family and friends would be taking the chairlift up the mountain at Smugglers' Notch to spread Sean's ashes. After the ski mountain event, many would be returning to Nancy's house, where my Bloody Marys would be served. Nancy was looking forward to the calming and closure of that gathering of close friends and family.

Katie and I drove to Smugglers' Notch Resort to meet up with Nancy and a dozen close friends and family several days after Sean's church service. We gathered near the Sterling chairlift and headed over to the sundeck by the lodge and waited for the ski lifts to close to the public, followed by the ski patrollers' "sweep," checking that all the skiers were off the mountain. After the slopes were cleared, one of the ski patrollers directed us to the chairlift. I had been holding the backpack containing an urn with Sean's ashes in it and passed it along to Wayne to carry up to the top of the mountain. Katie and I shared a chair and as it ascended to treetop height, I was reminded of my fear of heights, one of the reasons I stopped snowboarding. I felt a knot in my gut, as the windy day amplified the fear and my empty feeling of grief simultaneously as the chair swung side to side. It was a perfect blue-sky day, the sun masking the hollowness felt by the dozens gathered to honor Sean at one of his favorite places. We descended the ski ramp stairs and walked a hundred feet toward the ski patrol cabin at the top of the mountain. Most of Smugglers' Notch's sixty paid and volunteer ski patrollers were beginning to converge there from different parts of the resort. They were all there to honor and spread the ashes of one of their own.

Many of the patrollers, including Wayne, made brief speeches. They spoke of Sean's enjoyment of the hardest job that he absolutely loved, this from a guy who spent twenty-nine years at sea as a commercial fisherman and captain and a dozen years as a vegetable farmer. One of the patrollers read a requiem for a ski patroller, modified specifically for Sean. He paused, to gather himself, encircled by his fellow ski patrollers. He said they were truly family, and that comes with the good days and the difficult days, like today. One of the crew made up stickers with a photo of Sean in his ski patrol parka with the mantra he created, which was in turn loved by the rest of the men and women in patrol: "Ski fast, take chances." It described how Sean lived his life, on the sea, farming, on his motorcycle, and on the mountain.

Nancy was handed the urn and was the first to spread Sean's ashes, followed by several patrollers, some family members, and myself. Some spread the ashes on the ground and some preferred to send them airborne into the windy day, the ashes heading from east to west. After the words were spoken and Sean's ashes spread, scores of red parka-clad ski patrollers skied down the mountain as one, like a flock of birds gathering up and flying south for the winter, making graceful turns, sinuously skiing in formation. We observed this beautiful display of dedication to one of their fallen family from the chairlift above, following the scarlet column down the mountain.

The patrollers headed to their lockers to change and get ready for the potluck BBQ party they were holding in Sean's honor, as our separate group of family and friends headed back for a smaller gathering with Andrew and his caretaker, waiting back at Nancy's place. Andrew and Carrissa prepared some cheese fondue fixings and snacks as I prepared batches of Bloody Marys, the same way my friend Max did (from the essay "The Irish Wake"), with V8, lemon, horseradish, olive juice, olives, and celery stalks, and of course, lots of vodka. Bill, one of Sean's friends and a former ski patroller, stopped by with his guitar and brought lyrics to the three John Prine songs played at Sean's service, "Beautiful World," "How Lucky Can One Man Get," and the song he rode out on, "Spanish Pipedream." Our small group sang harmony along with Bill on lead vocal and guitar. It was a magical moment, celebrating a unique life, at the end of a beautiful day.

Two months before he died, Sean asked me to write the story of his life. I had only known him for a dozen years since he met my friend Nancy. Ten of those twelve years he courageously battled cancer and lived his life to the fullest. Despite the doctor's terminal prognosis, Sean's end came faster than he or any of us were prepared for. I think we all thought he would beat all the odds at the end in Sean-like fashion. I instead chose to write about the lives he touched and how he died. Sean died as he lived, with courage, candor, and with dignity, always on his own terms. I am honored to call Sean my good friend.

Sean Hayes

I Just Lost a Good Friend Today

© Jim Ryan

I just lost a good friend today
I was in the woods tapping trees
I felt like I'd been gut punched
And brought down to my knees

I needed to be close to him
I played his music that day
I got pretty sauced and cried
But he wouldn't want tears on his grave

I just lost a good friend
I just lost a good friend today

You laughed when you shouldn't have
At his profanity-laced jokes
And weaved all his fishing tales
While he drank White Russians and smoked

He helped the disabled,
The autistic, those who couldn't speak
He said it made him a better person
He helped them ski down mountain peaks

I just lost a good friend
I just lost a good friend today

Whistling Up In Ghostland

His closest people were with him
On his very last day
They sat around him, beside him
Held his hands as they prayed

It feels like a legend has passed
Maybe not in the traditional sense
Sean was a fisherman, a farmer
It doesn't make any sense

I just lost a good friend
I just lost a good friend today

At the moment he died
The radio tuned to the country station
John Prine's Spanish Pipedream
His favorite song, came on

The song about a topless dancer
With something up her sleeve
Sean got the last laugh
It was his parting deed

I just lost a good friend
I just lost a good friend today

Dandelion Wine

Newport, Vermont

February 2025

The medium's eyes met mine from twenty-five feet away. Her look gave me a very strange feeling. She looked spooked, which in turn spooked me. It seemed clear this medium had the special gift of intuition I was seeking at that moment. My choice was made. I approached her scheduling assistant and was excited that Carmen, the spirit guide, had availability right away. I quickly tried to get my person's, Katie's, attention at a nearby craft goods table. I wanted a witness to the reading and someone to help me process what might unfold during it.

Larv and Ted invited us to have dinner with them at their place, a hillside home overlooking the lake in Newport, just a handful of miles from the Canadian border. I searched Google to see if any out-of-the-norm events were scheduled for the same day we were to have dinner. The four of us were always on the lookout for esoteric events and out-of-the way places where unique characters might hang out. Ted and Larv often headed to Salem, Massachusetts, to celebrate Ted's Halloween birthday among the witch lore and Wiccan worshippers. A psychic fair in Newport popped up in the search engine on the same day we were scheduled to head there. It felt obvious we should attend; I was pulled to it. Before I could text my enthusiast-for-the-odd friend Larv, she beat me to the punch and, in synchronicity, suggested we should go to the same fair. Katie and I had attended a few psychic and medium events and were intrigued by what had unfolded at those readings, so she was totally on board with the idea.

The four of us met up at the Psychic and Medium Fair in an old gymnasium along the shores of Lake Memphremagog. Individual tables and booths lined the perimeter walls where the gym bleachers were pushed closed, and more tables arranged in rows filled the center. Katie and Ted were pulled to the artisans' tables filled with handcrafted earrings and necklaces, homemade hats and gloves, dream catchers, pendulums, and lavender sprays made of flowers grown at a local lavender farm. After visiting the various booths and tables, we converged in the back corner where the psychic and medium guides were set up. There were numerous offerings for tarot and angel card readings, Reiki healing, sound baths, massage therapy, and psychic, spiritual, and medium readings. Larv and I decided we were going to get individual readings. She chose tarot cards, and I had trouble deciding between two different psychic-medium readers, until my eyes met Carmen's.

The only information I initially gave Carmen was my first name, as Katie grabbed the seat next to mine. On the table between us lay a laminated homemade chart with the word "Universe" at the top, a circle of the alphabet letters, another circle of numbers, the words "yes," "no," "funny/LOL," and "I love you," on the sides—guardians of love and light, guides of healing and peace, and in each of the four corners, the words "air," "fire," "earth," and "water." At the center of the chart was a drawing of the head of a raven, which Carmen described as her spirit guide. Just to the side of the chart were several cylindrical-shaped pendulums made of different gemstones and crystals, each tapering to a point with a small chain attached. With her arms raised, Carmen closed her eyes and intoned a confident and seasoned request, inviting only spirits of love, light, and positive energy to attend our session. I told her not to hesitate to share any and all information with me about the messages she was receiving from the other side.

In the first five minutes of a scheduled fifteen-minute reading, Carmen confided to me that the strange glance she had given me earlier was because she "saw" another head next to mine that looked similar to me. Not surprisingly, her first question was about an older person who looked like me, a male relative, a father or grandfather. She was receiving signs of some sort of family confrontation over money and assets. It almost felt to me like a jumble of messages occurring concurrently; apparently, it was exactly that. She was feeling multiple spirits associated with me, all eager to come in and visit at the same time. They were fighting for attention from Carmen, and also from me. Anthony[1] describes spirits being both individual and in the collective simultaneously as collective consciousness,

---

1. Anthony, *The Afterlife Frequency.*

when communicating to loved ones in the material world. The spirit communication began to clarify. There was the presence of someone struggling for breath, someone not long for this world. Carmen looked directly in my eyes and said, "Prepare yourself for heartache." She felt I would be in emotional pain in the coming weeks or possibly days, sometime very soon.

Carmen shared that, for her, communicating with those on the other side was often like playing charades; she must piece together what they wanted to express to her clients. She felt the strong presence of a dog. I asked if the dog's presence was from one already "in spirit." She said it was a dog who had already died or one who was going to die very soon. She put her hands on her chest and said she was feeling the presence struggling to breathe, something terminal. I shared with Carmen that my previous dog, Alfred, had similar symptoms to what she described, and I had felt his presence after he died. I glanced at Katie and said I hoped it wasn't our current dog, Quinny. I urged Carmen to continue, even if the information she was about to convey might be painful for us to hear. She reaffirmed that heartache was in my very near future, and it could be more than just one event. Her dire words lingered.

Carmen then turned to her chart and dangled a pendulum, purple in color and made of amethyst. It was used to assist in spelling out names, or symbols, or important numbers being conveyed by the spirits present. She first tested the pendulum and asked it to start moving; it did. Then she asked it to stop moving at the center, and it did exactly that. She held her pendulum by its chain steady over the center of the chart and asked the spirits what they wanted to share with me. The pendulum started slowly swaying and moving to the letter *R* and then *I*. Carmen asked if the letter could be the name of someone I was close with who recently passed, a female. I looked at Katie and said yes, it was my Aunt Rita, who passed about a year and a half before.

Rita was like a second mom to me; we were close, and she had previously come to visit me after she died (described in the essay "Whistling Up in Ghostland"). Carmen was "seeing" a smiling presence, Rita singing and dancing. Carmen described Rita as a wholesome soul. She said she was happy on the other side; she mentioned a beach setting. She said she was no longer in pain and that her hair, which she couldn't properly care for in the end, was now beautiful again. I shared with Carmen that Rita did in fact love to sing and dance, that she had a second home in Florida close to the beach. Rita struggled for the last ten years or so of her life physically and mentally from Parkinson's disease and a series of small strokes. Rita conveyed to us in that session not to worry about her and that she regularly visited her husband, a reference to my Uncle Billy, and asked us to let Billy know she loved him and was nearby. The Rita spirit said she visits him at their home in the form of a raven, Carmen's animal spirit guide. Uncle Billy later acknowledged that groups of ravens had been visiting as of late.

Carmen recentered her pendulum over the chart, and it began to swing in a small circle again. This time the pendulum headed to the letter *S* and then *E*. There was no doubt who it was this time. It was my friend Sean. Sean died almost exactly one year before (described in the essay, "I Just Lost a Good Friend Today"). The last two weeks of Sean's life, he was at home on hospice. I spent nearly every one of those days with him. It was Sean's turn to come in to say hello. Carmen described this spirit as very strong and determined. She shared that he was laughing, swearing, and telling jokes. That was Sean, for sure.

Carmen was then seeing images of the Boston Red Sox, a

player or maybe a big fan? That male soul was playing cards. He was a dancer with a first name beginning with a *J*. That was Grandpa John (described in the essay "Strange Things Happening"). He and Grandma Nell were regular ballroom dancers, and he was a big Red Sox fan.

Carmen mentioned an older woman was coming in now. She had an older-sounding name beginning with an *E* or *A*. She had a very big garden she tended to while on Earth, and her gardening was more than just a hobby, it was her livelihood— she needed to garden to survive. It was Eva, whose farm I now live on (Eva's story is described in the essay "My New Old Friend"). Eva's spirit shared she had been heartbroken when her husband, Frank, died. She conveyed to Carmen that I was good to her and helped fill the void Frank's death left in her. Carmen said Eva still walks the land on our farm. That statement gave me comfort, knowing Eva approved of my continued stewardship of "our" soils and land.

Carmen said she sensed I had a very strong spirituality, reaffirming that I was intuitive, that I had certain healing gifts and abilities to communicate with those on the other side. In a combination of sharing her own thoughts and those conveyed to her by the spirits visiting me, she said I needed to have more confidence in nurturing those gifts. Carmen then spun her spirit chart around and passed it across the table to me. She asked me to select one of her several pendulums. I chose one made from white quartz. She told me I should ask the spirits to make the pendulum move, and I did; it started to circle. She asked me to ask the spirits to make the pendulum stop moving and center; it slowed to a stop over the center after I asked them to. Carmen then encouraged me to ask the spirits anything I wanted. I asked which spirits were still in the room with us. My pendulum first moved toward the letter *R*, recentering itself after I acknowledged the name, and then *S* again. Rita and Sean were still here.

As Carmen suggested we begin wrapping up the session, the pendulum I was holding began to head toward the letter *P*. Carmen was carefully watching what this spirit was spelling out. Carmen said the letter *O* and then *P* again. She asked me, "Who is Pop?" I paused, shocked at this revelation. Carmen described this person as male, pig-headed, never wrong, angry, and a grumpy old man. Carmen clarified that these descriptions of Pop were of him when he was in the living world. She said he had been healed now and was seeking reconciliation from the spirit realm.

Pop was my grandfather, my mother's dad, who had died twenty years before. He was also my Aunt Rita's father. Pop immigrated to Ellis Island from Calabria, Italy, when he was five years old. He shared stories of being called a "guinea" and "wop" and being spit on by other kids growing up as he learned how to speak English. He graduated from high school, married my grandmother, and enlisted in the US Army Air Force as a navigator. He served with the other air crewmen searching for German subs up and down the Atlantic seaboard during World War II. He wore his lieutenant uniform proudly.

Pop and I were very close throughout my life. He and my grandmother spent time with me and my brothers growing up, with long weekends at their home, spending summer days going to the nearby ocean, walking from their house to a neighborhood town park to feed the ducks and geese in the pond, playing cards and board games, and always challenging us mentally with quizzes on longer car rides. Upon recent reflection, I realized the relationship between grandparents and grandkids, my grandparents and me, can be one of the few bonds that is truly an exchange of unconditional love, unburdened by the day-to-day parent-child relationship of good days and challenging ones. That relationship is often easier and freer, and one that could easily shield his difficult personality.

Pop was a complicated person. Perhaps his patriarchal upbringing and being bullied as a child formed the basis for some of the toxic masculinity Carmen described in the person my mother and grandmother knew, rather than the man I remembered. His behavior toward me offered a glimpse of the person he *could* be. Many in my family did not speak to him, especially toward the end of his life, when he needed them the most, as his health declined. He had been emotionally abusive toward my grandmother in their relationship and toward my mother growing up. My mother never forgave him for how he treated her as a child and still held a deep-seated resentment. But she was reluctant to share any of those details of her traumatic experiences with my brothers and me, only that she was mistreated by him emotionally.

My grandparents had a mercurial relationship, with several separations. On one such occasion, I played mediator between them, leading to their reunion. He never let me forget my efforts to reunite them. Despite his flaws, he deeply loved my grandmother. After a severe stroke and brain surgery landed her in a nursing home, Pop visited her daily for nearly three years until she died, to brush her hair, caress her, and keep after the nurses whom he thought were providing insufficient care. He was devastated by her death, and he died shortly thereafter. Pop was another of my regular visitors from the other side. He had previously only come to me in my dreams. This was his first visit during daylight hours. He clearly wanted me to know he was with me. And in that session with Carmen, he asked for forgiveness, not from me but from my mother, through me. I found myself playing mediator once again, but this time one of the parties involved was living and one was in the spirit world. I realized the head Carmen saw beside my own that resembled me had been Pop's. I later wrote a song to help me process the complicated relationship between Pop and my mother and me (see A4: "If Your Heart Could Only See").

A moment later, Carmen was getting something new, something different. A new spirit was making its presence known, this time as she was holding the pendulum again. She turned to her assistant and asked if anyone else was scheduled and the assistant said no. Carmen said, "Good, let's continue the session." The pendulum swung to the letter *L*. She asked me about that letter and name. I paused to think for a moment, but nothing came to mind. The spirit was persistent; they wanted it to be known that they were there in the room, especially to me. They then communicated with Carmen visually. She clearly saw a bright yellow flower. Then she clarified her visualization: it was a dandelion. I stammered, "Oh my God." I stared off, toward the window, just behind and above Carmen. I began to cry. I tried to hold the tears back, so I could get my words out. I couldn't. Another cathartic cry, this time in public, in front of Carmen and her assistant at the fair, with Katie at my side. I couldn't get myself together for a minute or two, despite my best effort, and grabbed a handful of tissues Carmen offered me. In between my tears, I said aloud and to myself, "You idiot! The *L* is for Lydia."

My momentary memory lapse I attributed to the fact that Lydia was my ex-girlfriend Christine's middle name, a name I called her only after we broke up. After that terrible breakup, we both needed a new start. When we reconciled as friends, I became James to her, and she became Lydia to me. It took me those awkward moments to connect those dots. She died in 2019 and has since been a regular visitor to me in spirit (described in the "You Made a Difference" essay). Carmen heard Lydia laughing as my light bulb went off, realizing it was her. I shared with Carmen and Katie that the not-so-subtle dandelion hint was a clear signal to me, and only me, that Lydia was there with us. During our long-term relationship, we picked dandelions and made dandelion wine on several different occasions. On one of those days collecting dandelions, and in a moment of spontaneity, I proposed to Lydia in a hayfield of dandelions in full bloom on a warm, sunny late spring day on the shores of Lake Champlain. It was a belated twelve years into our relationship. Better late than never, she must have thought. She joyfully accepted my proposal, but we never followed through and got married. We broke up a year later.

Years after the hayfield proposal, I had entirely pushed that memory to the deep recesses of my brain, until Lydia reminded me about it on a phone call in the last months of her life, as she struggled with cancer. At the time of the phone call, she had known, but kept secret, that she was not long for this planet and instead wanted to share a memory and a laugh with me. At first, I didn't recall the memory in that phone call, until Lydia disappointedly nudged me after I failed to pick up on several dropped hints. Lydia's dandelion prompt from the other side reminded me of my prior memory lapse. Shortly after that call, I found an empty wine bottle I had stored away in my garage, with one of our homemade labels dated 1999. That belated recall of the proposal moment and finding the dandelion wine bottle inspired me to write the song "Dandelion Wine," about the proposal never fulfilled, and Lydia's death soon after the call. Now, Lydia was probably laughing from the other side at my second lapse of memory about the field of yellow flowers.

I was reeling. I felt shell-shocked, stunned, but happy at all my spirit visits. The scheduled fifteen-minute session lasted well over an hour. I left Carmen a generous tip and asked for her business card and said I needed a follow-up session with her soon. It was the first time all "my dead" visited me simultaneously, all vying for my attention through the conduit Carmen. They collectively asked me how I would like to receive their future messages for me. I replied that the ways they are currently communicating were working just fine: through lucid dreams, clairsentience, and my proactive summoning of them through music and natural settings. Carmen asked if I had my own pendulum and I affirmed that I did. She encouraged me to make my own board of letters, numbers, and symbols, like hers. Carmen reiterated I had the gift of intuition and mediumship and could even be a death doula, someone who assists people with dying. But I needed to better hone those skills, be open to it all, have confidence in it, and when in doubt ask my spirit guides to come in to assist me.

After that session with Carmen, my lifelong fear of death loosened its grip around me, ever so slightly.

"The" bottle of dandelion wine dated 1999 (photo credit

Whistling Up In Ghostland

Jim Ryan)

Dandelion Wine

© Jim Ryan and Dave Keller

We stopped at the field, on our way
Late afternoon, warm spring day
Picked dandelions, in full bloom
Field by the lake, sun setting soon

Laid down in the field, all through the hours
Picked a bouquet, of those bright yellow flowers
In the moment, Lord, I proposed
You said yes, as the tears streamed down
    your nose

Chorus
Well, the moment in the field, etched in
    my mind
That day forever, frozen in time
Homemade label, May '99
I stare at this bottle, of dandelion wine

It's been six months now, since you passed away
I think about you, every day
We never got married, I'm not sure why
I can still see you, in that springtime sky

Repeat chorus

Whistling Up In Ghostland

Scan the QR code to listen to the song,
performed by Dave Keller

Prepare Yourself for Heartache
Bear Swamp Farm, Vermont

February 2025

Back home from the Newport Medium and Psychic Fair and Carmen's spirit reading, Katie and I noticed Quinny's occasional cough had returned, and she had a strange breathing pattern. We didn't think it was anything too serious in prior weeks; perhaps the kennel cough. When we awoke the next day, her breathing had deteriorated further. We exchanged glances, confirming we were witnessing the very scenario Carmen had described the previous day. It was late Sunday; we agreed we needed to get her to the vet first thing on Monday, the next day. The vet's office sensed our urgency and squeezed us in at 9:30 that morning.

Quinny began to quiver in the car looking out the window as we got closer to the vet's office. She always hated going to the vet, despite their gentle care for her. It could have been the smell of other pets' fear that caused her trepidation. After we got her into one of the exam rooms, Dr. Ryan listened to her breathing with his stethoscope and felt around her chest. He shook his head and said she indeed was struggling for breath; this was not a good sign. An X-ray revealed she had retained more than three liters of fluid, likely an indicator of cancer. Dr. Ryan said he could drain the fluids after sedating Quinny to help relieve her breathing difficulties; we agreed. The draining was successful, and she began breathing normally again. But follow-up X-rays and blood work revealed what he suspected, an aggressive, fast-growing lymphoma. Quinn did not have much time left. Katie and I did not want any part of putting a fourteen-year-old dog through chemo and radiation, which could only extend her life by weeks or a few months. We realized Carmen's spiritual reading foretold this exact event; we were just not expecting it to come so quickly, and with it the devastating heartache she predicted for us had arrived.

Dr. Ryan said one option was to put Quinny to sleep right there on the spot, since she was still sedated from the draining procedure. After some discussion back and forth, Katie and I decided we weren't comfortable with that option. We couldn't allow our beloved Quinn to die in the sterile environment of the vet's office she had always dreaded, even in her current unconscious state. We didn't want her to be in any discomfort or pain, and after the fluid draining, she wasn't. We were going to take her back home, to *her* home. The vet had previously agreed he could come to our farm to put her to sleep when her time had come, which was unfortunately now. Our vet typically does not make house calls to euthanize pets, but he made the exception for us since we had been coming to his office for nearly a decade and a half with Quinn. We scheduled that dreadful appointment for three days later. It was one of the most difficult and emotional three days of our lives.

Quinny seemed to be relieved to get out of the vet's office and to be back home. We would at least have some time to say goodbye to her in familiar and comfortable surroundings. She had been my steadfast and constant companion for fourteen years, especially after the pandemic hit five years before and I was able to work from home full-time and then take an early retirement. She was my sidekick. Those last nights of her life, I slept beside her on our guest bed downstairs, since she could no longer make it up the staircase to our bedroom.

The full Snow Moon at Bear Swamp Farm (photo credit Jim Ryan)

The full Snow Moon illuminated the downstairs bedroom all night long. I awoke in the middle of the night, rolled out of bed, and lay beside Quinn on her dog bed. She was wide awake with her head fully upright, her ears pointing upward, staring into my eyes. I had gotten into the practice in the last six months of having these special moments with her, as if I knew her end was coming soon. As I was petting her body and rubbing her chest, I assured her I loved her with all of my heart, as unconditionally as she loved me, and thanked her for being part of our family and for all our fun times together. I had tears in my eyes as I told her things were going to be okay. And I said we would always be together. I asked her to please visit me when she got to the other side to let me know she was all right, just as I had said to my Aunt Rita on the day she died. I asked Quinn if she understood what I was saying, and she looked right into my eyes and blinked both her eyes slowly and intentionally shut and then back open. It was our way of communicating.

On her last day, she woke me up at 5:00 AM, as she normally did, thumping her tail against the wooden guest room door. Quinny and I went outside into the cold early morning as the full moon descended near the horizon. Two gray cirrus clouds brushed horizontally across it, as it set in between the silhouette of spruce and balsam crowns on the hillside behind the house. We gazed at the moon from the same back porch where we shared many a sunset together, me on a porch rocking chair and Quinny on her dog bed looking out. Katie and I gave her some of her favorite foods and treats, pieces of roasted chicken, tuna fish, and GravyBones dog biscuits. An hour or so later, we walked out the front door to watch the sun rise between The Ledges and Judevine Mountain as Quinn tasted the snow, as she loved to do, on this calm, sunny bluebird winter day. She stared out at her familiar surroundings and her home for many minutes, apparently taking it all in, one last time. Katie and I took turns getting down onto our knees and wrapping our arms fully around her, hugging her as we did on most days, but this time it was to say our final goodbyes, as the vet called to say they were on the way.

Hardwick, Vermont, May 2025

Rebecca Anne LoCicero is a psychic-medium from Connecticut. She ventures to the Northeast Kingdom in Vermont twice a year to host medium events at the three-hundred-seat Hardwick Town House. Rebecca was made famous for her appearance on the Netflix series *Surviving Death*. This was the second time Katie and I had gone to see Rebecca in person. This time, we brought our eighty-seven-year-old spiritually enlightened neighbor, Betsy, along with us. Betsy's husband died twenty-five years prior. The three of us regularly talk of things woo-woo, like our shared thoughts on life after death and communication with those on the other side, including Betsy's husband.

It had been two and a half months since Quinn died on the full Snow Moon in mid-February. A good friend of Katie's had a portrait of Quinny painted for us and I made a regular habit of talking to her, via this portrait, nearly every day. On this day, earlier in the afternoon, I asked Quinny to come visit us at the medium event.

It was a rare sunny late afternoon in the year's otherwise rainy spring, the first weekend in May. The sun's energy seemed especially poignant when I noticed the last rays of the day peeking through some upper theater window in a strange rectangular-shaped reflection onto the stage's pastoral painted curtain above Rebecca's head as she was addressing the audience. I simultaneously felt a tingling sensation throughout my body. I whispered into Katie's ear, "Quinny is here," as she sat beside me in Hardwick's Victorian-era Town House auditorium. Katie shushed me and gave me a sideways glare, as if to say, "Don't interrupt the speaker." But recognizing the importance of what I was experiencing, I said it again, "Quinny is here, in this room right now." Katie seemed more receptive to my statement the second time around. Rebecca opened the event and established the ground rules for the evening. "Don't feed the medium by giving her too much information."

Rebecca wandered around the room as the various spirits she invited in began to gather closer to the evening's attendees. I intentionally grabbed a middle aisle chair, as I normally do, where I can stretch out my fidgety legs, with Katie and Betsy to my right. Rebecca was heading up our aisle from the stage on the way to read someone's spirit message directly behind us. Just as Rebecca was walking past us, she looked Katie and me in the eye, smiled, and said, "Someone left the dog door open," then positioned herself two rows behind us.

Rebecca began reading that person's message from their spirit. Rebecca then migrated back to us. Her steady gaze seemed to include both of us, and she said she was feeling the strong presence of a dog, a female dog who recently passed. She asked if this was meant for us. We both said yes, as the person holding the microphone came in closer. We answered more than yes or no only to fill in the voids in Rebecca's messages, but tried not to feed the medium, as she requested. Rebecca said she was surprised to have a pet come in because it was extremely rare for her. She said this dog was our soulmate, that Quinny was expressing gratitude to us for taking her in and giving her such a good life. Rebecca described visions of Quinn running around on our farm and mentioned a very special homemade food bowl and a luxurious bed. Katie and I nodded in agreement. Katie, a very talented potter, made Quinn a special bowl. Just a few months before she died, we had purchased her not one, but two, deluxe six-inch-thick dog beds to ease her achy older bones. I called them princess beds.

Rebecca accurately recounted we'd had to call someone, a female vet, to our place to euthanize Quinn and this decision had been extremely difficult for us. Tears started welling up in our eyes as Rebecca spoke, and we were the center of attraction for the two hundred attendees. Rebecca passed along a message from Quinn that she knew it was the right decision for us to make, as difficult as it was. Rebecca shared that Quinn was grateful to be home with us in the end. Rebecca then said Quinny was buried next to several other animals. We acknowledged we had her buried in the front yard next to a deceased lamb, goose, and cat. Quinny didn't mind the company.

Quinny (photo credit Kristy Gerdo)

Carmen's surreal spiritual reading a few days prior to Quinn's sudden death and my recent experiences with the dead and dying confirmed for me in no uncertain terms that there is something for me, or us, something on the other side after we die. After spending my life in fear of my own death, I felt confident I would, at the very least, be taking my consciousness with me when I died. I would have the ability to visit with those remaining on Earth. I would be Whistling Up in Ghostland, riding in on my songs to visit with those I love.

Now Among the Stars

© Jim Ryan

Mediums and psychics
Talk to those who died
They can see what I can't see
There's a good chance, I'll cry

Are they sending signals?
To say they're alright
To help guide them home
A tunnel of bright light

Chorus
There's so many I'd like to speak to
All those so dear to me
My good friends and loved ones
There's so many I long to see

Matter and energy
Particles and waves
Now among the stars
They'll never fade away

Sometimes when I'm by myself
I stare up at the sky
With our music playing loud
Their faces appear up high

Repeat Chorus

Epilogue

Bear Swamp Farm, January 20, 2026

The northern lights, January 20, 2026 (photo credit Jim Ryan)

I scurried into my bedroom and reached into the closet for one more layer of Smartwool long johns, a wool sweater, a pair of Darn Tough socks, and wool pants. Wool was my weapon of choice for protection against the biting cold that is mid-

January in northern Vermont at night. A frigid blast of weather had settled in. Katie was doing the same, layering up, as we added warm gloves, neck gaiters, and winter hats, to our arctic outfit. Our neighbor Bradley had just texted, "The northern lights are out," with a teaser photo of their magnificent display. We felt a sense of urgency to see nature's light show before it disappeared. It was the first time in sixteen years living at Bear Swamp Farm that we had a chance to catch the elusive event. The landline rang as we were on the way out the door. It was Brandon. I was expecting his call. We were planning to go over the logistics of his trip to Vermont the next weekend for a visit, along with his girlfriend, Leanne. I told him that the northern lights were out and I would have to call him back. I hung up and dashed out the door.

In our remote valley, we are fortunate to have no sources of light pollution in our three-hundred-and-sixty-degree view. The northern lights' green, pale yellow, red, and purple illumination was going strong; I watched them dance and dart. They were alive! I once characterized the northern lights to a friend who had never seen them before, as tornadoes bouncing around the night sky with rainbows within them.

When I reached Brandon about an hour later, he broke the news. Joe had died. He wasn't sure of the exact cause of his death. He'd only found out the night before, and Joe's family was still piecing things together. Joe was only thirty-one years old. I sat in my chair searching for words. I could only muster "Fuck!" which I repeated, over and over again, as Brandon continued to speak.

During and immediately after the call with Brandon, I

started thinking about Cat, Joe's chosen nickname because of his love of caterpillars. The Joe that Leanne, Brandon, John, and I loved was in our inner circle of friendship, a fellow Ghost Rider. John is Brandon's ex-wife's nephew. They remain close friends, despite Brandon's divorce. John and Joe, similar in age, were best friends.

Cat deeply loved his parents and his brother, also named John, and sister Katie. They are a tight-knit and religious family, always helping and supporting one another. Joe was raised Catholic but was also on a quest to find his own spirituality, spending time at local Buddhist centers and monasteries as of late.

I recalled Joe's musicianship, his singing and playing harmonies with his brother John. Joe was an accomplished player on the guitar, piano, and drums. Cat always carried his guitar with him, even on remote canoe camping trips to the Adirondacks.

Cat had a way of reaching each of us at deeper levels through channeling, as Brandon would say, directing just the right song, book, or poem, to each of us individually or collectively, at just the right moment. Joe especially worshipped the musician, Trevor Hall, who sprinkles spirituality, nature, peace, and love in his lyrics. Once, Joe dedicated the song, "The Green Mountain State," to me, being the only Vermonter in the group. He sang and strummed along on his guitar with the rest of the Riders in audience in Brandon's black shack on the Ghostland mountaintop, our sacred space. He sang, "There's a way, there's a way, there's a way." We were all deeply moved as we sang along in harmony.

Joe brought us the spiritual cleansing ceremony of smudging all the items and lands that we hold sacred with sage, palo santo, and cedar. Smudging is a sacred act of clearing negative energy and promoting healing and health. The idea of the smudge sled was born. My crazy companions desired a first-for-humanity feat, a shock-and-awe event. They did not fail. Brandon, Joe, John, and Leanne schemed this surprise performance for the Mountain Jam event atop Ghostland. A smudging on steroids. After an evening of performances, poetry, theatrics, fire dancing, wood sculpture burning, and music, Mountain Jam merrymakers, including myself, were told to prepare ourselves for something special. A fiery finale.

Ghostland ablaze (photo credit Brandon Dennis)

In a bonfire-illuminated darkness, Brandon led the preposterous procession atop his 1971 Massey Ferguson 135 tractor with his farm wagon hitched to the back, pulling his cargo of comrades, and attached behind them, the homemade smudge sled. John, the artist among our group, handcrafted the sled with two wooden runners, a piece of roof tin for the floor to withstand the heat, and wooden painted half suns on the sides painted yellow and orange. John and Leanne stood on either side shooting bottle rockets and Roman candles high in the air above the spectators' heads, screaming and shouting with joy, as Joe sat beaming, seated on a milk crate behind a full drum set of bass, snare, tom drum, and cymbal. Joe played solos and fills on the back of the cart to the audio of the Doors song "The End." Brandon, the ecstatic operator, encircled the crowd with the tractor, howling in wolf-like fashion to the party participants' delight. The smudge sled, filled with dried white cedar boughs, now on fire, cleansed the entire mountaintop, while awestruck revelers were serenaded by the hypnotic crescendo of Joe's drumming and the whistling screeches and thunderous booms of firework explosions.

In recalling this spectacle, I was reminded that participating in insane antics with like-minded friends in nature makes me feel most alive. The memory of a joyous Joe playing the drum set on the smudge sled being pulled by the tractor, cleansing Ghostland, will linger in my mind for the rest of life.

I opened the back porch door and walked down the stairs into the yard to tell Katie about Joe, the northern lights still shimmering above. The invigorating frigidity reminded me of our winter adventure to Ghost Rider Island in Maine, nearly three years ago to the day (described in the essay "4,000 Weeks"). I wandered further out in the yard to get a better look at the night sky, as Katie retreated to the warmth inside. It seemed as if the movement of the colorful clouds of light were like lips moving. They were trying to speak to me. Just then, I noticed what looked like a set of eyes hovering above the horizon, in the middle of the light show. The eyes morphed into a face-like shape. I asked the sky, "Is that Joe in there?" My body warmed and tingled all over, despite the numbing cold. The warmth extended from my throat, down my chest, and into my stomach, as if I took a stiff swig of cognac. I felt his presence, if only for a moment.

Joe had always described his spiritual place, his place of divinity, and the mysterious as the numinous. I can visualize Joe now sitting on a mountaintop overlooking a lake in the numinous, playing his guitar and singing his favorite songs from the heart. If any of my friends in the spirit world were to come in and visit me, riding in on a song (as described in the essay "Whistling Up in Ghostland"), it would be Joe. I hope he visits soon and often.

Joe "Cat" Lacourt (photo credit Leanne Nabinger)

Sources

Abbey, Edward. *Desert Solitaire: A Season in the Wilderness.* McGraw-Hill, 1968.

Anthony, Mark. *The Afterlife Frequency: The Scientific Proof of Spiritual Contact and How that Awareness Will Change Your Life.* New World Library, 2021.

Budbill, David. *Judevine.* Chelsea Green Publishing, 1991.

Budbill, David. "A Place in Mind." *Northern Woodlands*, Autumn 2014, 80.

Burkeman, Oliver. *Four Thousand Weeks—Time Management for Mortals.* Farrar, Straus, and Giroux, 2021.

Dumpert, Jennifer. *Liminal Dreaming: Exploring Consciousness at the Edge of Sleep.* North Atlantic, 2019.

Durkheim, Emile. *The Elementary Forms of the Religious Life.* 9th ed. Free Press, 1995.

Fenwick, Peter, and Fenwick, Elizabeth. *The Art of Dying.* Continuum International, 2008.

Jung, Carl. *Synchronicity: An Acausal Connecting Principle.* The Collected Works of C. G. Jung, vol. 8. Princeton University Press, 2010.

Kean, Leslie. *Surviving Death: A Journalist Investigates Evidence for an Afterlife.* Crown Archetype, 2017.

Keltner, Dacher. *Awe: The New Science of Everyday Wonder and How it Can Transform Your Life.* Penguin, 2023.

Maslow, Abraham H. *Religions, Values, and Peak-Experiences.* Penguin, 1970.

Maslow, Abraham H. *Toward a Psychology of Being.* Van Nostrand, 1962.

Meadows, Kenneth. *The Medicine Way: A Shamanic Path to Self-Mastery.* Element Books, 1990.

Miller, William, and C'de Baca, Janet. *Quantum Change: When Epiphanies and Sudden Insights Transform Ordinary Lives.* The Guilford Press, 2001.

Tolle, Eckhart. *A New Earth: Awakening to Your Life's Purpose.* Penguin, 2006.

Williams, John. "Life is Short. What are You Going to Do About That?" *The New York Times Book Review.* August 11, 2021.

Appendices

A1: The Songs (in the order they appear)

- **Saline Skies**—by Lizzy Mandell and Jim Ryan; performed by Lizzy Mandell.
- **St. Patrick's Day, 2002**—by Jim Ryan and Joanne Breidenstein.
- **Met You Sooner**—by Dave Keller and Jim Ryan; performed by Dave Keller.
- **Come Home to Me**—by Dave Keller and Jim Ryan; performed by Dave Keller.
- **Judevine**—by Lizzy Mandell and Jim Ryan; performed by Lizzy Mandell.
- **My New Old Friend**—by Lizzy Mandell and Jim Ryan; performed by Lizzy Mandell.
- **The Irish Wake**—lyrics by Jim Ryan.
- **Angola**—lyrics by Jim Ryan.
- **You Made a Difference**—by Scott Graner and Jim Ryan; performed by Scott Graner.
- **4,000 Weeks**—by Dave Keller and Jim Ryan; performed by Dave Keller.
- **Strange Things Happening**—by Dave Keller and Jim Ryan; performed by Carly Harvey.

- **Whistling Up in Ghostland**—lyrics by Jim Ryan.
- **I Just Lost a Good Friend Today**—lyrics by Jim Ryan.
- **Dandelion Wine**—by Dave Keller and Jim Ryan; performed by Dave Keller.
- **Now Among the Stars**—lyrics by Jim Ryan.
- **If Your Heart Could Only See**—lyrics by Jim Ryan.

A2: Behind the Scenes—The Musicians and the Songs

On Songwriting, by Jim Ryan, lyricist and author

To me, songs should tell a story. The lyrics within these pages tell stories of profound experiences that have happened to me and to those close to me over the last two and a half decades. All the songs share an underlying current of things mystical, as I view my life as a spiritual journey. The lyrics describe themes about the Universe, time and space, inner peace, death, grief, deep connections with friends, nature, and sense of place. There are real people behind the characters in these songs, both living and in the spirit world.

Equally important in telling a story through song is the music. The gifted musicians and songwriters featured here established the tone, setting, tempo, phrasing, instrumentation, and solos. Their musical choices help express the emotion and passion of the song. I had the privilege of being in the studio and getting the chills as these songs were recorded and the lyrics were brought to life. As with most artistic collaborations, once my lyrics were recorded by musicians, we shared songwriting credits: Just as the musicians have offered changes to my original lyrics during the recording process to help the songs sing better, I have also provided input into the music, especially the emotion I was trying to create.

Music can make you laugh, make you cry, give you chills, and help you recall special moments in your life. To me, music is spiritual.

Lizzy Mandell—singer, songwriter, and guitarist

Our unscripted adventure to Death Valley had all the ingredients for a great story song: a majestic landscape, outdoor adventure, colorful and unique minor characters, the camaraderie of the main characters, personal epiphanies, and collective resolution. It took me a full eighteen years to write about our story in detail. But within days of returning from the trip, I was able to write my first draft of the lyrics that became "Saline Skies" and shared them with my Saline copilots, Kevin, Pat, and Brandon. It was one of the first times I used lyrics to help process one of my life's profound lucid experiences. Many more soon followed.

I enrolled in a singer-songwriter workshop at the Summit School of Traditional Music and Culture in Montpelier, Vermont, facilitated by locally renowned musician, producer, and studio engineer Colin McCaffrey. Lizzy Mandell, a relatively unknown musician at the time, and a handful of other songwriters also attended. I was struck by Lizzy's beautiful, soulful voice and natural songwriting skills. I was the only lyricist in the room, as others wrote both lyrics and their music. Colin tasked the attendees to write a new song each week and perform it for the group. Attendees offered up constructive criticism of songs, if desired by the performer. After one of the sessions, I approached Lizzy with my admiration for her work. I couldn't believe she was not yet "discovered." She thought I was a talented lyricist.

Colin approached Lizzy to record some of her songs in his

studio. She agreed. It was Lizzy's first album, *Made for Flying*. Lizzy asked me if she could record two of my song lyrics for her album, with Lizzy co-writing the music. I enthusiastically said yes. Lizzy went on to win Vermont Tammie awards for best Vermont songwriter and best album of the year in 2012 for her debut album, a well-deserved honor. I was deeply humbled that two of the songs I had co-written with Lizzy, "Saline Skies" and "Judevine," were included in this critically acclaimed recording.

I wrote the lyrics to the song "Judevine," inspired by the mountain that bears its name, which I see out my front door every day. I learned early on in my lyric writing that I loved to intertwine nature and emotion. It is a recurring theme in many of my songs. In my teenage years, I loved the acoustic song by Led Zeppelin called "The Rain Song." It described emotion through the seasons with vivid visuals of natural settings. It was that song that first inspired me to write lyrics back in high school. I reached deep within for a similar balance in writing "Judevine."

I invited Lizzy to Bear Swamp Farm shortly after I purchased it. I had shared my original lyrics for "Judevine" with her, and she was equally excited to get a sense of what the farm and surrounding landscape looked and felt like. She came over on a cool spring late afternoon and sat with me at my kitchen table with the woodstove warming the room. She brought her guitar with her to share a rough melody she had been working on. As Lizzy tuned up the guitar and then began playing in her finger-picking style and overlaying her vocals, I felt a twinge of magical energy. Lizzy was sitting at my kitchen table singing the words I wrote to describe this special place, while both of us looked out at the forest and fields.

When crafting the "Judevine" lyrics, I tried to reflect on my literal and figurative personal journey as I was in the process of buying the farm, with its many ups and downs and my determination to succeed in that mission. Reaching back to my teenage inspiration, I intertwined emotion with a beloved landscape and my yearning for it to be my new home.

Lizzy Mandell

Dave Keller—singer, songwriter, and guitarist

A decade after the memorable experience shared in "Wish I Met You Sooner," I thought an Irish destination wedding in Spain would be a very original narrative to tell through song. "Met You Sooner" is one of those fact-fiction hybrid songs. I shifted the setting from Spain to Ireland, only because I didn't feel like I had enough song-lyric real estate to describe the destination wedding and two different nationalities. I replaced the Mediterranean scenery with Irish imagery. I changed the bride's name to Magdalene; I thought it would sing better than Siobhan. I grabbed the name after watching a Netflix movie, *The Magdalene Sisters*, set in Ireland. Siobhan did have long black hair falling to her waist, as I depicted in the lyrics.

I kept all the real-life happenings about the bus ride abduction, the "Wild Rover" song, and hanging out with the bride and groom on their wedding night. But I left out the participation of Michael-David, the bride's brother. I thought it would have been too complicated, and besides, it would have been more intriguing if it were just me and the bride. I slightly changed the last chorus's language to reflect the narrator now saying, "I wish I met you sooner" to Magdalene. It was meant to be a subtle transition and to show how the narrator remains intrigued by the possibility of that statement despite the passage of time. For the record, we never kissed or held each other's hand. That part of the song was fiction. Siobhan's cryptic comment, "I wish I met you sooner," would serve as the heart of the song, somewhat ambiguous and yet so curious and alluring. Many listeners of the *Free Now* album ask if this story really happened. The answer is, yes, and no.

Dave Keller and I had been friends for several years when I approached him in 2020 about taking guitar lessons. Dave is a three-time Blues Music Awards nominee who tours nationally and internationally. My guitar lessons with Dave at the onset of the pandemic on Dave's front porch quickly transitioned to us working on songs together. I felt grateful to collaborate musically with him. Dave ever astonishes me with his ability to come up with rough chords and melody for my lyrics right there on the spot, as he did in this instance.

When I shared the lyrics for "Met You Sooner" with Dave, he thought he could come up with a melody and did. He even added a verse to my original lyrics, the last verse of the song, about the narrator coming back to the States, still reflecting upon the bride's curious statement while sipping some Jameson. The song narrator, and the listener, are left forever wondering, what if?

In January 2026, Dave and I went back into the studio, this time at the brand new Destroy Audio studio, in Wolcott, Vermont. Dave recorded our songs "Come Home to Me" and "4,000 Weeks" for the book, with Zeph Courtney as producer and engineer. It was just Dave and his 1966 Guild T-100D guitar and vocals. Simple, beautiful, and soulful!

Scott Graner—singer, songwriter, and guitarist

In the days and weeks following Lydia's death, winter transitioned to mud season. The rain came, absorbed by the softening snow, and the streams turned to chocolate milk. The dreary darkness and bare trees set the stage for this true-to-life-story song, perfectly reflecting how I was feeling on the inside.

As February transitioned to March, my personal transition began. The sun appeared, we sprang ahead, and daylight grew each day. I slowly began overcoming my grief and channeled it toward my self-awakening, as this new person inside me emerged after the emotional carnage. As I wrote and spoke from the heart with those closest to me during this period, I realized sometimes when you hit rock bottom, physically, mentally, and spiritually, you are also the most vulnerable, and therefore most open to personal transformation. I wanted my lyrics to reflect my emotional transition from hitting bottom to deep heartache, and then to gratitude, to hope. And, as with most of my songs, that positive resolution is reflected in the chorus.

I met Scott Graner at a Northern Vermont Songwriting group meeting. Scott sang and played his guitar with deep passion, from the heart. I was seeking the intensity of feeling that Scott's writing and performing offered. I approached him about collaborating on "You Made a Difference." He came up with just the emotion I was looking for in writing and performing the music.

Carly Harvey—singer and songwriter

I brought my lyrics for "Strange Things Happening" to Dave Keller and he came up with a melody on the spot. I was deeply moved by his acoustic guitar chord progression and voice. I grabbed my cell phone and recorded the rough demo, and Dave jotted down the chords for me to take home.

Dave called me two days prior to our recording session at Colin McCaffrey's studio, The Greenroom, and left me a very excited voicemail. His good friend and fellow musician Carly Harvey, "DC's Queen of the Blues," was in town to perform some shows with him. Dave asked me if I was interested in having Carly perform a song for the *Free Now* album. I admit, I had never heard of Carly before, so I googled her website and YouTube channel. I was blown away that this serendipitous alignment of talent was arriving at my door. I enthusiastically said, "Yes, please," to Dave. I re-sent the rough demos of a few songs Dave and I previously worked on and asked him to share them with Carly. She picked "Strange Things Happening."

While Colin and Dave switched the studio mic setup for Dave's acoustic guitar in The Greenroom, I sat at the kitchen table with Carly. I asked her if she had any questions about my lyrics for "Strange Things Happening." I asked if she wanted some background or my thoughts on the emotional feel of the song. Carly said she would love to hear the story behind the song.

I conveyed to Carly the emotional arc I was going for in the song: deep sadness at the time of death expressed in the verses, the building of emotion in the pre-chorus, leading to a happier tone of relief in the chorus, celebrating dying relatives successfully making it to the other side. It was a song about the afterlife and spirituality. That conversation led Carly to share some of her experiences with the deaths of loved ones and her spiritual intuitiveness. We were spiritual brethren, and I really wanted someone with a strong sense of spirituality to sing this song. Carly was absolutely the right performer. We were deeply immersed in conversation when Colin called us back into the studio.

With Carly standing behind a vocal mic, they began a practice take of the song, which Colin fortuitously decided to record. She started her deep vocals softly, almost inaudibly, then she slowly raised both the volume and emotion, going deeper into the song. Carly's vocals were stirring. I teared up. The emotion of this song, more than any other, was still very fresh and deep. Carly struck a chord deep within me. It was a practice take, with some parts Carly really liked and a couple of parts that she didn't like as well.

They dove right into take two. Carly's voice was more confident, with deeper emotion and expression. The second take was nearly perfect. Colin worked his editing magic and after fifteen or twenty minutes had a new track for us to listen to. All I could say was "Wow." Dave, Colin, and I were in awe. Carly was magic in the studio. After Carly's studio appearance, Dave overlaid the electric guitar and Colin added bass and some slide guitar. We brought in Jay Gleason, the talented drummer from the Dave Keller Band to play drums on all of Dave's songs on the *Free Now* album, including "Strange Things Happening."

Colin, Carly, and Dave (photo credit Jim Ryan)

Colin McCaffrey – songwriter, musician, producer, and studio engineer

Colin and Dave both served as president of Friends of the Winooski River, where I initially met Colin in my days as a watershed coordinator with the Vermont Agency of Natural Resources. It is perfectly clear why the Times-Argus has called him "Central Vermont's go-to guy for recording, producing, performing, and all things musical."

Colin's insight into convincing Lizzy to record her debut album at his Greenroom recording studio was spot on. Colin's fingerprints were evident on the entire *Free Now* album. Colin, a well-known recording artist in his own right, brought all his talents to the table, playing a wide assortment of instruments: guitar, bass, mandolin, and fiddle, as well as singing harmony for almost all of Lizzy's tracks and lead vocal and co-writing on "Northbound Rail." Colin spent countless hours in his studio getting the feel of the album right, layering in different instruments and in its mastering. Colin and Lizzy recently completed a stunningly beautiful follow-up album called *To the Moon*, recorded at The Greenroom.

A3: Saline—A Poem by Brandon Dennis

Saline © Brandon Dennis

The moment is right for the final round about.
She is a woman, and I can still feel her sunburnt
  heart.
I had to muzzle my passion to hold my promises
  together.
But that flame still dances with the western sky.

In the peak of ancient sunset, I will honor the fire
  that sets the soul a glow.
Boundless space touches land to sky.
A waterless air lays all the rocks bare.

The crossroads have now been traversed.
Rattlesnake leads a bugle to the morning light.
Descending upon mystery to discover the hot
  springs delight.
The reality exceeds the rumors and delusions of
  wonder.

In friendship we bound onward to the
  mountain.
Ascending across the rising folds of bedrock into
  the sky.
Making my creed to forge the foundation of
  conviction.

In honesty we lay our souls wide open.
The risks are well worth the rewards of kinship.
Right or wrong we gain trust.
We give trust as we maintain our faith in the
goodwill that we share.

To the newborn and the beloved, I'm bound in
fidelity.
I will honor the gifts bestowed by those sacred
vows.
The children play within the safety of our grove.
Their imaginations are unbridled in the sanc-
tity of our honored commitment.

Turning from the East I descend that mountain
Westbound.
Among friends I enjoy the camaraderie of
mineral spirits.
Dancing among us, the velvet winged sentries of
night dine upon the winged delights
hovering
above the pools.
Soon I am alone with the sound of spiraling bats.

The sound of wing and wind in my ears.
It's time to turn and face their flight.
Speed and risks are whizzing past my eyes.
The future is now dead, and the present circum-
stances spin out of control.

I have to embrace fearlessness to honor the beauty
of the being whole.
And in my trust in faith of perseverance, I am
struck straight out by an aerial acrobat.
In shock I have to regather my courage.
Face it I must, because you can never hide from
the truth.

Stretching my arms out I challenge the skills of
winged ones.
Staring straight ahead I feel a blur of motion.
I find myself at peace with a truce I have
declined with fear.

Behind me I can hear the West walking around
me watching.
With friends she approaches me open to the
moment.
Our eyes engage and our words test each other.
Sentence by sentence we move delicately toward
each other.

In awe and wonder I try and communicate with
the mythical.
With fearlessness I convey the honesty of this
journey.
Openly we dance around each other with the
trust of children.
Tonight, we are playmates in the moment.

The beauty I walk upon is a woman.
In Death she has taken on a human form.
Sometimes I speak to her like I am speaking to
the desert itself.
Skirting around the fringes of madness we break
the connection of sanity.

Conversation with the desert goddess is like
speaking in a pool.
Submerged in the sulfur waters I get my answers
in the starlight.
Embrace all of those divisions and don't betray
your heart.
Breath deep and inhale her message.

Everything is wide open and I'm really listening
now.
No choices ever really had to be made when
you're stomping on your soul.
Saline says it's all good, so set your armor down.
In Deeper Death there is an oasis to be found.

—Diamondback

A4: If Your Heart Could Only See ©
Jim Ryan

There's a man who sits beside me
It's the man the mediums see
He's in the spirit world now
And he looks a lot like me

Fought in the Second World War
Flying the Atlantic seas
The greatest generation
Not so great to family

Chorus
Now he visits in my dreams
He comes knocking on my door
Death made him a better person
So much better than before
He begs for your forgiveness
And he asks this through me
You're only hurting yourself now
If your heart could only see

As a father, he was cruel
As a grandfather, so kind
You say you can't let it go
Have mercy, isn't it time?

In the end, no one gave a damn
When he died, he died all alone
You said he got what he deserved
But he tells me he's atoned

Chorus
Now he visits me in my dreams
He comes knocking on my door
Death made him a better person
So much better than before
He begs for your forgiveness
And he asks this through me
You're only hurting yourself now
If your heart could only see
Please forgive him, forgive him for me

About the Author

Jim Ryan recently retired after a three decade career in the field of natural resource management and watershed protection and restoration. When Jim is not writing, he spends his free time volunteering for his favorite causes, practicing Reiki, traveling, and recreating in nearby mountains, lakes, and streams. Jim lives on a small farm in northern Vermont.

For more information, please visit: https://jimryan.org/

www.ingramcontent.com/pod-product-compliance
Lightning Source LLC
Chambersburg PA
CBHW051816150726

47998CB00001B/179